NEW ORLEANS
Classic
APPETIZERS

NEW ORLEANS
Classic
APPETIZERS

Recipes from Favorite Restaurants

KIT WOHL

PELICAN PUBLISHING COMPANY

GRETNA 2008

Camille and Sofia. Imagine the little bites.

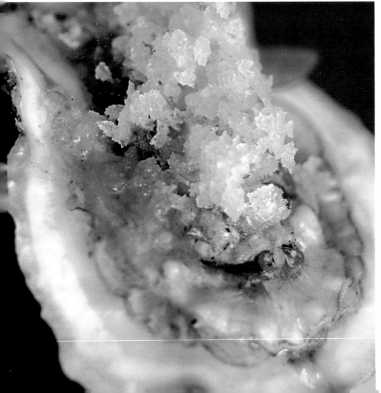

CONTENTS

Never Eat Anything Heavier Than You Can Lift
~Miss Piggy

Let's agree on something immediately: You can call them appetizers, hors d'oeuvres, canapés, amuse-bouches, antipasti, mezedes, tapas, finger food, small bites or nibbles. Whatever you call them, everybody loves them. They stimulate the appetite by design, but may also satisfy your appetite as an entire meal … a good one.

New Orleanians claim, rightly, that we eat more appetizers because we party more. We party at home, in friends' homes, on balconies and patios, parks, backyards, and on the neutral grounds (what we call the medians that run down the middle of streets). We party in hole-in-the-wall cafes, festivals, elegant restaurants and hotels — from low-down to high-falutin'.

We're so proud of our party food that many of us wear a few extra pounds of it at all times just to remind us how good it is. (Joe Cahn, an old friend and tailgate aficionado, claims that we're overweight as ballast, so we don't blow away.) Here in the Big Easy, it's a safe bet that the extra pounds are not from just any food. They've been earned honestly by eating the best food in the world.

In New Orleans, restaurant dishes listed as appetizers are so popular many diners prefer to make a meal of several and ignore the main event. One group of young chefs stop (on their night off) at several restaurants around town, sampling the appetizers and teasing their colleagues who are still working.

To be sure, chefs love to show off for other chefs. Now you can also take a star turn by using some of the recipes provided by these chefs. We've tested, tasted and enjoyed them for you first.

Here are 50 recipes covering appetizers from Restaurant August to Zea — from grand old culinary gals to feisty young upstarts. Most recipes are designed to serve as a bite or be presented as a first course.

Get your appetite ready for recipes from La Petite Grocery, Peristyle, Bistro Daisy, Herbsaint, Arnaud's, Bayona, Commander's Palace, Cochon, Café Adelaide, Vizard's, Zea, Antoine's, Galatoire's, Dickie Brennan's Bourbon House, Joel's Fine Catering, Food Arts, Cuvée, La Côte Brasserie, and other magical bistros, cafés, and restaurants.

Imagine shooters that don't make you silly. Sublime crawfish or shrimp in sake cups. Raw oysters served in a shot glass, dancing in flavorful finery. Contemplate shrimp in a number of guises, beef carpaccio, deviled quail eggs capped with caviar. These are a few of the exciting new recipes, along with old favorites such as cheese straws, crab meat au gratin, puffs stuffed with bits of savory or sweet delights — and so much more.

When my friends and I were young and exploring the business world and French Quarter of New Orleans, we made theater or art gallery openings, receptions, cocktail parties and special events a Friday evening adventure and a dinner of appetizers.

We frequently were offered food we couldn't afford, and much less could cook ourselves. New things to eat were at times peculiar to our way of thinking, but they were free. Later on we began entertaining on our own balconies and patios, reinventing family classics, sometimes including a little last-minute necessary creativity from cans, boxes and leftovers depending on our budgets.

Leftover chili with a sprinkle of grated cheese on toast points was a huge hit when chili was the only thing we had around. The guests thought chili triangles a little odd, but they ate them, a lot of them. Odd is not the same as tasteless.

We also discovered that chips, breads, vegetables, or other edibles could function as dipping or scooping implements, making washing dishes a tad simpler. (Who could deny the wisdom of that?)

A note: During a reception preceding a meal, or as a first course, culinary authorities say that preparing three to six bites per person is a good rule of thumb. A cocktail party or a reception with no meal to follow would average 10 or so pieces per person. See what works for you. This is supposed to be fun.

Since Miss Piggy commands us never to eat more than we can lift, she thinks appetizers of any kind are perfect. The question is, how many of them can we lift? Here in New Orleans, we're good at heavy lifting.

~Kit Wohl

For nearly 70 years, Vonderhaar's grocery was a fine-foods institution in New Orleans at the Magazine Street address that is now La Petite Grocery's. Vonderhaar's also delivered, which made them a hit around here, especially at my house. Those were the good old days.

For the good new days, Joel Dondis renovated the converted space into a clean-lined, French-style bistro with menus to match. Dondis also operates Joel's Fine Catering and Sucré, a confectionery and pastry shop that's also on Magazine Street.

La Petite Grocery's interior is lined with pressed-tin ceilings and dark woods, but food is the focus, as it should be in this location.

ROASTED GARLIC AIOLI

YIELDS: 1 cup

2	egg yolks
1 clove	garlic, minced
1 teaspoon	kosher salt
1/4 teaspoon	black pepper
1 tablespoon	lemon juice
1 cup	canola oil
1/4 cup	olive oil

DIRECTIONS

Blend all ingredients together except the oil. Slowly pour both oils in and blend well.

LA PETITE GROCERY
LOUISIANA BLUE CRAB BEIGNETS
WITH ROASTED GARLIC AIOLI

Savory beignets are a takeoff on the better known sugar-coated variety. La Petite Grocery makes theirs using crab meat, but shrimp and crawfish substitutions would also be delicious.

SERVES: 6, each 1 1/2 to 2 ounces

BEIGNET FILLING

1/4 pound	jumbo lump crab meat, Louisiana blue crabs preferred	1/2	French shallot, finely minced
1/4 pound	mascarpone cheese		kosher or sea salt to taste
2 tablespoons	chopped chives		freshly ground black pepper, to taste

DIRECTIONS

Thoroughly mix all ingredients in a bowl. Shape into small bite-size balls, with a diameter about that of a quarter, and chill.

BATTER

2 quarts	peanut oil*	1 cup + 1 tablespoon	cornstarch
1 cup	Wondra instant flour, preferred, or all-purpose flour	1 tablespoon	baking powder
		1 cup	beer

A good-quality vegetable oil also may be used.

DIRECTIONS

Mix all ingredients in a large bowl until blended, but batter should be lumpy.

In a large saucepan, heat oil over high heat to 375°F.

Dredge the chilled crab meat balls through the batter. Taking care to coat them completely. Using a slotted spoon, place them one at a time in the oil so they are not touching. Be careful to avoid being burned by splashing oil.

Fry the crab balls until golden brown, about 2 to 3 minutes. Remove them with a slotted spoon and drain on paper towels. Serve with roasted-garlic aioli for dipping.

REMOULADE
CRAB CAKES
WITH CREOLE-MUSTARD SAUCE

YIELD: 24 to 36 crab cakes

CREOLE-MUSTARD SAUCE

1	egg yolk	1/4 teaspoon	freshly ground black pepper
3 tablespoons	Creole mustard	3/4 cup	canola oil
1 teaspoon	kosher or sea salt	1/4 cup	olive oil

DIRECTIONS

Place all ingredients except the two oils in a blender and combine them. Slowly pour in each of the oils and blend well. If the sauce is not to be used immediately, refrigerate it in a covered container until serving time. Arnaud's bottles a magnificent Creole mustard and Arnaud's Sauce Remoulade, available at www.arnauds.com.

CRAB CAKES

1 pound	jumbo lump crab meat, Louisiana blue crabs preferred	2	large eggs
1/4 cup	small-diced red bell pepper	3/4 cup	unseasoned bread crumbs
1/4 cup	small-diced green bell pepper	1 tablespoon	worcestershire sauce
1/4 cup	small-diced yellow bell pepper	1 teaspoon	Tabasco sauce
1/2 cup	small-diced yellow onion	1 tablespoon	Creole mustard
4 tablespoons	vegetable oil	1/2 cup	mayonnaise

DIRECTIONS

In a small mixing bowl carefully pick through the crab meat to remove shell fragments. Heat 2 tablespoons of the oil in a medium-size sauté pan over high heat and sauté the bell peppers and onion until the onion becomes translucent, about 4 to 5 minutes. Remove the peppers and onions from the heat and allow to cool.

In the bowl with the crab meat, combine the peppers and onions and all the other ingredients, but use only 1/4 cup of the bread crumbs. Mix everything well, but gently, to avoid breaking apart the crab meat lumps. Once the mixture is well combined, allow it to sit for 5 to 10 minutes to ensure that as much liquid as possible is absorbed by the bread crumbs. With a spoon, or your hands, gather enough of the crab meat mixture to shape into balls about the size of a ping-pong ball. Set aside.

In a large skillet, heat the remaining oil over medium heat. While the oil is heating, place the remaining bread crumbs into a large mixing bowl. Roll the crab cakes in the bread crumbs until they are well coated and gently shake them to remove excess crumbs.

Once the crab cakes have been breaded, flatten them slightly and gently place them in the heated oil, being careful not to burn yourself. After approximately 2 minutes, turn the crab cakes to ensure even cooking. They should be golden brown on all sides, and the entire cooking time should be between 4 and 5 minutes. Serve the warm crab cakes with the Creole-mustard sauce on the side, which should be at room temperature.

The best thing next to Arnaud's is Remoulade. The grande dame's little sister restaurant is a blue jeans and red beans kind of place.

In 1994 Archie A. Casbarian converted a building at the end of his properties on Bourbon Street. It is named Remoulade, in honor of Arnaud's sauce and serves a food festival with the best of New Orleans home cooking and fresh seafood.

Guests may belly up to the fresh Louisiana oyster bar to have a few dozen opened in front of them or dine at tables scattered throughout the brightly lit, classically French Quarter-styled establishment.

FRIED SPINACH GARNISH

The late Warren LeRuth delighted everyone when he introduced fried parsley as a garnish. Parsley stays colorful when fried, is crunchy, and is a nice surprise. This recipe produces the same bright note.

Preheat oil to 350°F in a skillet or an electric deep fryer.

1 bunch	small fresh spinach leaves
1 quart	vegetable oil

Clean spinach with running water to remove any sand or grit. Dry with paper towels. Use small leaves or tear into 2-inch pieces.

Place the leaves in the oil without crowding. Fry only for a few seconds, watching carefully. Do not brown. Remove with slotted spoon and drain on paper towels. Use as garnish.

In a city known for its culinary excellence and abundance of fine restaurants, few establishments have achieved worldwide acclaim. Arnaud's stands as a monument to the enduring allure of classic Creole cuisine, as well as to the excitement of gustatory innovation.

This New Orleans restaurant is a leader of the culinary Old Guard and serves tradition today with a menu of classics with a thoroughly contemporary accent. Within its beautifully restored, historic walls, one can sample dishes created on the premises — succulent Oysters Bienville and Arnaud's famous remoulade sauce, to name only two.

Arnaud's lasting success can be attributed in part to the constancy of its owners. It has had only two families as owners since its establishment in 1918.

The Casbarian family infused the restaurant with tradition and flair and shepherded its growth as a magical place to savor the full experience of a meal. They are dedicated to the fundamentals of Arnaud's heritage, keeping one foot in the past and the other a step ahead with a menu that bursts with seasonal flavors and the fun that is the soul of New Orleans and the legends that shaped it.

Their son and daughter, Archie Jr. and Katy, have joined proprietors Archie and Jane Casbarian.

ARNAUD'S
CRAB CLAWS À LA PROVENÇALE

Arnaud's proprietor Archie Casbarian takes special pleasure in this dish. The crustacean's delicate flavor is accented with butter and anisette liqueur for a sweet, bite-sized morsel that is hard for even the strongest man to resist. The claws are served on crostini, fairly thick slices of a French baguette or other bread that also has a rather thick crust and is toasted.

SERVES: 60 bites or 6 appetizers

1	French baguette, cut into 1/2-inch diagonal slices	1/3 cup	Herbsaint, preferred or Pernod anisette liqueur
60	Louisiana blue-crab claws, boiled	1/4 teaspoon	kosher or sea salt
1/2 pound	unsalted butter	1/4 teaspoon	black pepper, coarsely cracked
6 cloves	garlic, very finely chopped	1	fireplace or kitchen match, the longer the better, to prevent burns
1/3 cup	finely chopped flat-leaf (Italian) parsley		

DIRECTIONS

Preheat the oven to 350°F and place the sliced baguette on a large baking sheet. Toast until golden brown, 10 to 15 minutes, and set aside until serving time.

If you have the entire crab claw, crack it and remove the large, round bottom shell, including the larger, moveable pincer. Carefully remove the remaining smaller pincer with the meat attached.

Place a large skillet over medium-high heat and add the butter. When it is melted, add the garlic and stir for 15 to 20 seconds, until aromatic. Do not allow the butter to break or the garlic to burn.

Add the crab fingers and toss gently, until they are coated in butter. Cook for 30 seconds, then stir in the chopped parsley. Place the Herbsaint or Pernod in a large ladle and ignite with the match. Drizzle the flaming liquor over the crab and cook for about 45 seconds, until the flames die down. Stir in the salt and pepper, and cook for about 20 seconds more.

Remove claws from heat and arrange them vertically in individual ramekins, meat side down, or on a large platter, with the pincer ends able to be held easily for eating. Spoon the remaining butter mixture from the pan over the crab claws. Place the ramekins on a small side plate and arrange the croutons around the rim, or place the croutons in a basket alongside the platter of claws.

ANTOINE'S

Chair de crabes au Gratin
crab meat au gratin

SERVES: 8
BÉCHAMEL SAUCE
YIELDS: 1 1/4 cup

3 tablespoons	unsalted butter	1	whole clove
3 tablespoons	all-purpose flour	1	bay leaf
1 cup	whole milk		kosher or sea salt to taste
1/4 cup	thinly sliced white onion		freshly ground white pepper, to taste

DIRECTIONS

This will be a white roux. It will be cooked only to remove the flavor of uncooked flour.

Melt the butter in a saucepan over low heat. Slowly add the flour, a teaspoon at a time, to the melted butter to form a paste, about 1 minute. When the paste begins to foam gently, stir for 1 to 2 minutes, being careful not to brown the roux. Remove from heat and set aside.

In a separate saucepan over medium-high heat, combine the milk, onion, cloves and bay leaf, and bring to a boil, about 4 to 5 minutes. Reduce the heat so the milk is simmering and gradually add the roux, whisking in 1 teaspoon of it at a time. Once the roux has been combined with the milk, allow it to continue to simmer for 1 to 2 minutes until the consistency thickens to the point where it will coat the back of a spoon. Whisk in salt and white pepper to taste. Strain the sauce through a fine colander to remove the cloves, bay leaf and pieces of onion. Use immediately.

Antoine's is treasured for its little quirks, which include a private entrance for locals and personal waiters who take reservations for their regular customers.

The generations of waiters also follow the generations of guests, in a continuous line of families joined at the table.

The sprawling buildings that Antoine's occupies also include private dining rooms specially decorated with festive memorabilia collected by members of New Orleans Carnival organizations, or krewes.

While tradition reigns at Antoine's, credit cards are now accepted, Sunday brunch is now served, and the menu remains in French, but with an English translation for each dish.

CRAB MEAT AU GRATIN

1 1/4 cup	béchamel sauce	4 tablespoons	grated cheddar cheese
2 1/2 cups	lump crab meat, Louisiana blue	4 tablespoons	grated Romano cheese
	crabs preferred	4 tablespoons	grated mozzarella cheese
	kosher or sea salt, to taste	1/4 cup	bread crumbs
	freshly ground white pepper, to taste		

DIRECTIONS

Preheat the oven to 400°F.

In a medium saucepan, blend the béchamel sauce and the crab meat together gently, so as to not break up the crab meat. Season the sauce with the salt and pepper, and heat the mixture over medium-high heat for 1 to 2 minutes. Remove the mixture from the heat and spoon it evenly into six small gratin dishes or ramekins.

In a small metal bowl, combine the cheeses and bread crumbs. Place 2 heaping tablespoons of the mixture on the top of each of the dishes. Place the dishes in the oven, and bake for 12 to 15 minutes, or until the top begins to brown.

Sheila and Stephen Bellaine's entertaining sense of humor extended for years to Mardi Gras, when they provided hot soup, other good eats and a place for a breather.

During the Carnival season, they hosted friends and family who would drop in during the long day of passing parades just a block off St. Charles Avenue. When that house was sold, Sheila and Stephen moved far from the parade routes, but they brought this special recipe with them.

Stephen is notoriously camera-shy, but he is an excellent accountant, and a master of the barbecue grill. He's just someone who ducks photographs.

Sheila, on the other hand, is photogenic and always has a big smile ready, whatever the occasion. She's most famous as the "laughing lady" on the original Semolina restaurant's radio commercials.

SHEILA AND STEPHEN BELLAIRE
Crab meat Pontchartrain Biarritz

SERVES: 36 bites or 6 appetizers

CRAB MEAT AND DRESSING

1 pound	jumbo lump crab meat, Louisiana blue crabs preferred
2 tablespoons	freshly squeezed lemon juice
2/3 cup	mayonnaise
2/3 cup	whipping cream, beaten but not stiff
3 tablespoon	finely chopped Bermuda onion, optional*
2 teaspoons	capers
	Louisiana-style hot sauce, to taste
	kosher or sea salt and black pepper, to taste

DIRECTIONS

Carefully pick any shell pieces or cartilage from crab meat lumps and discard. Gently toss crab meat with lemon juice and let stand covered in the refrigerator for 30 minutes or more and drain.

*Stephen does not use onion for this recipe. The addition is ours, so go with your conscience.

To make the dressing, mix all ingredients except crab meat in a medium-size bowl and refrigerate, covered, for at least 1/2 hour, until very cold.

Mix the dressing with the crab meat, taking care not to break up the crab meat lumps.

ARTICHOKES

2	artichokes, stem trimmed
	toast points or crostini for garnish

DIRECTIONS

In a covered saucepan, steam the artichokes for 30 to 45 minutes until a leaf pulls away easily from each. Drain the artichokes upside down in a strainer or colander and cool them until they can be easily handled.

Split each artichoke lengthwise in half and remove its inner choke and some of the deepest leaves, creating a cup in each of the four halves. Discard the chokes and leaves you removed. Take the two less attractive of the four artichoke halves, pull away all of their tender, but sturdy, leaves and set them aside. The sturdier leaves will be topped with the crab meat and dressing.

Shortly before serving, remove the crab meat with the dressing from the refrigerator and place a teaspoon of it onto each artichoke leaf. Also, fill the cups in the two remaining artichoke halves with the remaining crab meat mixture and surround the halves with filled artichoke leaves.

Serve with toast points or crostini for scooping crab meat from the cups in the artichoke halves.

CRAB MEAT RAVIOLI

In 1980 Chef Goffredo won the Crab Meat Olympics in San Francisco with his subtle Crab meat Ravioli.

SERVES:

BÉCHAMEL SAUCE

1/2 cup	milk	1 pinch	white pepper
1 tablespoon	butter	1 pinch	red pepper
1 tablespoon	all-purpose flour	1	egg yolk
1/4 teaspoon	salt		

DIRECTIONS

Melt butter and flour, salt and pepper. Cook 2 or 3 minutes, whisking all the time. Add cream gradually, whisking to avoid lumps until sauce thickens. Let simmer until reduced to 1 cup. Set aside to cool. This will be used in the crab meat filling.

CRAB MEAT FILLING

1/2 cup	chopped green onions	2 tablespoons	chopped parsley
1 tablespoon	butter	1 pound	lump crab meat
1	egg white	4 tablespoons	cracker crumbs

DIRECTIONS

In a medium-size saucepan add the green onions and butter. Sauté until vegetables are softened, then cool. Place the béchamel sauce atop the crab meat filling when the filling is placed in the ravioli dough.

RAVIOLI DOUGH*

4 cups	all-purpose flour	1 cup	water
1 pinch	salt	2 large	eggs, slightly beaten

DIRECTIONS

Place the flour and remaining ingredients into a bowl. Work with hands or a wooden spoon until a dough forms and can be made into a ball. Knead for 5 or 6 minutes and set in a bowl to rest. After an hour, put dough on a floured board and roll to a thickness of about 1/16 inch.

Place crab meat balls about 1 1/2 inches apart on a sheet of pasta dough. Paint area between the balls with water and top with a second sheet of dough. Form ravioli by pressing around each ball to form a seal. Dust with flour and cut into squares. Boil for 5 minutes in rapidly boiling salted water.

Any easy dodge is to use wanton or egg roll wrappers instead of pasta dough.

Master Chef Goffredo Fraccaro founded La Riviera Restaurant in 1969. Following Hurricane Katrina the popular Italian restaurant did not reopen.

His appetite for civic and charitable events is enormous. He and La Provence's late Chef Chris Kerageorgiou cavorted through special events as a comedy duo, cooking and laughing together.

The Chef's Charity for Children at St. Michael's school holds a special place in Chef Goffredo's heart and in the children's hearts he has a special place, too.

SAUCE

1 cup	heavy cream
2 ounces	softened butter
to taste	salt and pepper
1/2 cup	freshly grated Parmigiano-Reggiano cheese

DIRECTIONS

Reduce the cream by one-third and season with salt and pepper. Whisk in the butter and serve over ravioli. Top with grated cheese.

Chef Anton's experience has given him the reputation and confidence to launch a refreshing new establishment. The restaurant's warm character is enhanced by the charming dining spaces fashioned from the original rooms of an Uptown New Orleans cottage.

CRAB MEAT AND ROASTED-GARLIC AIOLI
OVER ROASTED BEETS WITH CHIVES AND CROUTONS

The buzz around town is Anton and Diane Schulte's Bistro Daisy–a happy showcase of bistro cuisine with a kicky personality and fresh local ingredients. Tenure at Peristyle and La Petite Grocery has given Chef Anton the chops to satisfy the most demanding local guest. Diane is gifted with the kind of gracious hospitality to welcome them.

SERVES: 6

ROASTED-GARLIC AIOLI

YIELDS: 1 cup

1	egg yolk	1 tablespoon	freshly squeezed lemon juice
8	garlic cloves, roasted	3/4 cup	canola oil
1 teaspoon	kosher or sea salt	1/4 cup	olive oil
1/4 teaspoon	cayenne pepper	1/8 cup	extra virgin olive oil
1/4 teaspoon	freshly ground black pepper		

DIRECTIONS

Blend all ingredients together except the oil. Slowly pour both oils in and blend well in a blender.

CRAB MEAT

12 ounces	jumbo lump crab meat, Louisiana blue crabs preferred	1/4 cup	thinly sliced chives
		1 cup	petit croutons
3	medium red or yellow beets	1/4 cup	extra-virgin olive oil
1/4 cup	vegetable oil		kosher or sea salt, to taste
1/2 cup	roasted-garlic aioli		black pepper, to taste

DIRECTIONS

Preheat oven to 400°F.

Place the vegetable oil in a small bowl. Roll the whole beets, skin on, in the oil and season with salt and pepper. Place the beets on a baking sheet and roast in the preheated oven for approximately 1 hour, or just until they are knife-tender. Remove the roasted beets from the oven and chill in the refrigerator until completely cold. Peel the beets and then cut into thin slices. In a medium-size bowl, gently fold the crab meat together with the aioli and chill.

To serve, place the sliced beets evenly at the centers of six chilled appetizer plates. Divide the crab meat into six equal servings and place on top of the beets. Garnish each plate with a generous amount of chives and croutons. To finish, drizzle a small amount of extra-virgin olive oil onto each plate. Serve cold.

PETIT CROUTONS

YIELDS: 1 cup

5 slices	white bread
2 tablespoons	olive oil
	kosher or sea salt, to taste
	freshly ground black pepper to taste

Preheat the oven to 350°F.

Remove the crusts from the bread slices and discard the crusts. Cut into 1/8-inch cubes.

In a medium-size bowl toss the cubes with the olive oil and season with salt and pepper to taste. Spread the bread cubes evenly onto a sheet pan, and place in the preheated oven.

Bake for about 5 to 7 minutes, or until the bread is evenly golden brown. Remove and allow to cool.

CHEF WARREN LERUTH
CRABMEAT ST. FRANCIS

SERVES: 12 to 16 appetizers

1/4 cup	dry white wine	1/4 teaspoon	cayenne pepper
1 quart	heavy whipping cream	1/4 teaspoon	freshly ground white pepper
1 pint	crab stock	1 1/4	teaspoon salt
4	bay leaves	1/2 cup	all-purpose flour
6 ounces	butter	4	egg yolks
1	large green onion, finely sliced	1 tablespoon	chopped fresh Italian (flat-leaf) parsley
2	large cloves garlic, chopped	2 lbs.	fresh Louisiana jumbo lump crabmeat
1/4 cup	chopped white onions	1/2 cup	unseasoned bread crumbs
3/4 cup	chopped hearts of celery		fried parsley as garnish
1/2 teaspoon	dried thyme		
	generous pinch celery seed		

DIRECTIONS

Preheat the over to 425ºF.

In a saucepan, bring the wine, cream, crab stock and bay leaves to a simmer and hold there. In a skillet over medium heat, melt the butter and sauté all the remaining ingredients until the vegetables are limp and translucent.

Add the flour to the vegetables and stir over low heat for about 5 minutes to make a blond roux. Do not let it brown. Whisk in the cream and stock mixture completely. Lower to just under a simmer, add the parsley and cook for about 15 minutes. Remove the bay leaves.

Whisk in the egg yolks, one at a time.

Place 2 ounces of lump crab meat in a ramekin or baking shell. Top with 1/2 cup of the sauce, sprinkle lightly with breadcrumbs and bake at 425ºF until the top is browned and bubbly. Garnish with fried parsley if desired.

FRIED PARSLEY GARNISH

1 bunch	curly or flat leaf parsley
1 quart	vegetable oil

Clean parsley with running water. Dry with paper towels. Remove long stems. Place the leaf clusters in the oil without crowding. Fry only for a few seconds, watching carefully. Do not brown. Remove with slotted spoon and drain on paper towels. Use as garnish.

The late Warren LeRuth, a seminal New Orleans chef, was secretive about his recipes and published only two small pamphlets containing them. LeRuth's in Gretna was the cuisine-changing restaurant that created a seismic shift in the late 60s and 70s, a haven of haute-Creole dining.

One recipe of major impact was his signature Crab Meat St. Francis. While it was not exactly a secret, it was not widely published.

According to Tom Fitzmorris, a New Orleans food critic and author, Warren once told him that the biggest thing he missed about not having the restaurant anymore was that he couldn't eat Crab Meat St. Francis whenever he wanted to.

Tom once attended a dinner in San Francisco where Lee LeRuth — Warren's son, who ran the restaurant for a few years until his untimely death in his 30s — cooked Crab Meat St. Francis. Tom watched and took notes. This is Warren's recipe, as observed and tested by Tom, who had also enjoyed it at the restaurant.

Marcelle Bienvenu loves the south Louisiana bayous and waterways almost as much as she does its products and cooking them. It is her heritage. Her accent flavors her comments as much as her garden seasons her creations.

She's been the go-to lady for many famous chefs, including co-authoring books with Emeril Lagasse and working with Paul Prudhomme at Commander's Palace. She's an author, commentator, and a Times-Picayune columnist. Marcelle has been a chef and operated her own restaurant.

SEAFOOD SAUCE

2 cups	mayonnaise
1/2 cup	ketchup
2 teaspoons	prepared horseradish
2 teaspoons	worcestershire sauce
2 teaspoons	fresh lemon juice
1/2 teaspoon	hot sauce

DIRECTIONS

Combine all of the ingredients in a mixing bowl and whisk well. Store in an airtight container in the refrigerator until ready to serve.

CRAWFISH BOULETTES

SERVES: 10 to 12

STUFFING

1 cup	vegetable oil or butter
3 medium	onions, minced
4 ribs	celery, chopped
4 medium	green bell peppers, seeded, and minced
5 cloves	fresh garlic, minced
1/2 cup	crawfish fat (if available, if not use 1/2 cup butter)
1 1/2 pounds	fresh Louisiana crawfish tails, shelled*
8 to 10 slices	day-old bread, soaked in water and squeezed dry
2 tablespoons	salt
1 tablespoon	freshly ground black pepper
1 tablespoon	cayenne pepper
1 cup	unseasoned bread crumbs
1 cup	seasoned bread crumbs
	leafy greens

Fresh Louisiana shrimp, cooked and shelled, may be substituted for the crawfish tails.

DIRECTIONS

Heat 1/2 cup of the oil or butter in a large, heavy pot over medium heat. Add the onions, celery, bell peppers and garlic. Sauté the vegetables until they are soft and golden, 8 to 10 minutes. Add the crawfish fat or butter and cook, stirring for 3 minutes. Remove from heat and set aside. Grind 1 pound of the crawfish tails and the bread together in a meat grinder or food processor.

Heat the remaining 1/2 cup oil (or butter) in a large, heavy pot or Dutch oven over medium heat. Add the crawfish-bread mixture, the cooked vegetables, salt, black pepper, cayenne and the remaining 1/2 pound of crawfish tails. Cook, stirring, for 5 to 8 minutes. Remove from heat and cool to room temperature, stirring it several times as it cools.

Combine the bread crumbs together in a small bowl and set aside. Preheat the oven to 375°F.

With wet hands, roll 1 tablespoon of the stuffing mixture into quarter-size balls, then roll on a generous amount of the bread crumbs, patting them gently to adhere to the stuffing. Place the balls on a large baking sheet and bake until the bread crumbs are a light golden brown, 15 to 20 minutes. Remove from the oven and set aside.

Serve on a platter of leafy greens with a side of seafood sauce for dipping. Have small plates or toothpicks nearby.

CHRISTINE MASON

CREAMY CRAWFISH AND ENDIVE

Nothing is easier to enjoy than a crunchy piece of endive blessed with a savory filling. It is the perfect finger food to be picked up and relished.

SERVES: 32 bites or 8 appetizers

1 pound	fresh Louisiana crawfish tails, cooked and shelled*	1 tablespoon	Creole mustard
1/2 cup	fresh crawfish tails,* cooked and shelled	1 tablespoon	whole capers
3/4 cup	mayonnaise	2 tablespoons	minced green onion or chives
3 tablespoons	ketchup	1/8 teaspoon	hot pepper sauce
		1/8 teaspoon	worcestershire sauce
		3	heads of endive

Fresh Louisiana shrimp, cooked and shelled, may be substituted for the crawfish tails.

DIRECTIONS

Set the 1 pound of crawfish tails and the endive heads aside.

Prepare the sauce by placing 1/2 cup of crawfish tails, the mayonnaise, ketchup, Creole mustard, capers, green onion or chives, and the hot pepper and worcestershire into a food processor and pulse briefly to mix well.

Place the remaining crawfish tails in a large bowl. While adding the sauce gradually, toss the tails gently until the desired consistency is reached. Refrigerate.

Cut endive heads 1/2 inch from the bottom and separate each leaf from the core. Wash each leaf and dry with paper towels. Set aside and chill.

Arrange the endive leaves on a serving platter or appetizer plates. Place 1 tablespoon of creamy crawfish into each leaf and serve.

Christine's sense of humor extended to joining our staff as a test cook for our first, the Arnaud's Restaurant Cookbook. We wanted someone who could not even boil water. If she could follow a recipe successfully, we conjured, it would work for anyone. Her first attempt was Shrimp and Scallops Eva, a heady success that won praise from friends and family.

That treacherous path led her to the prestigious New England Culinary Institute, where she received her BA with honors in Hospitality Management.

My dear friends, her grandparents Earlene and Bernard Mason, have just barely forgiven me for interesting their only granddaughter in the culinary arts. She is creative, energetic, and returned to help with this effort, although now she now knows her way around a kitchen and tries to manage everyone here. In that, she is not successful.

Robert Barker's sense of humor is as expansive as his appetite for creativity. As culinary director of New Orleans Classic Appetizers, *he was able showcase his favorite appetizer — his novel, locally inspired crawfish or shrimp shooters. They will dazzle your guests.*

Robert supervised the recipe testing for this book and translated "chef speak" into home-kitchen language and instructions. His talents for food presentation also prompted us to bring him into our photography sessions.

As an executive chef, Robert is as guilty as the next guy of assuming that home cooks know the shorthand and mysteries of a restaurant kitchen.

He always joined in our efforts to write recipes that can be prepared with limited experience and equipment. He welcomed outside opinions, solicited and otherwise. Most of them were embraced and appreciated. Our editor, Gene Bourg, was the final, solicited opinion.

The result is that the recipes in New Orleans Classic Appetizers *are easy to prepare with basic kitchen equipment, from products readily available from good grocery stores or specialty shops, and are as delicious as you'd expect them to be.*

After you've prepared this appetizer, take your bow. But also thank Chef Robert.

CHEF ROBERT BARKER
CRAWFISH SHOOTERS

A delightful, delicious and grand surprise for your guests. This unusual and elegant teaser can be prepared a day or two ahead of time and heated at the last minute before serving.

SERVES: 12 shooters or 6 appetizers

1 pound	fresh Louisiana crawfish tails, cooked and peeled*	1/2 tablespoon	aniseed
1 pound	shrimp shells	1/2 tablespoon	cracked black peppercorns
1 ear	corn in husk	1 cup	orange juice
12	chives	1	carrot, peeled, roughly chopped
2 tablespoons	unsalted butter	1/2 gallon	water
1/4 cup	fresh ginger, peeled and grated	1/2 cup	Kikkoman aji mirin
2	French shallots, roughly chopped	1/4 cup	granulated sugar
		1 cup	heavy cream
1/4 cup	minced garlic	1	lime, juiced
2	celery stalks, minced	1	whole clove
		1 bunch	cilantro, roughly chopped
1 tablespoon	coriander seeds	1 bunch	mint, roughly chopped

Fresh Louisiana shrimp, cooked and shelled, may be substituted for crawfish in this recipe.

DIRECTIONS

In an 8-quart stockpot, combine shrimp shells with all ingredients except crawfish tail meat, corn, chives and butter. Bring to a boil over high heat.

When a boil is reached, reduce heat to medium and slowly simmer mixture for approximately 1 hour.

Remove the stockpot from the stove and strain the liquid through a fine-mesh sieve or colander over a bowl. Discard solids.

Return the stock liquid to the stockpot and bring to a slow simmer over medium heat. Reduce the stock liquid by 1/4 or until slightly thickened. This second simmer should take 1 hour.

Thirty minutes before the reduction is complete preheat the oven to 350°F. Place the whole ear of corn in the oven on a baking sheet and roast for 20 minutes.

Remove the corn from the oven, and cool. Remove the husk from the corn, and using a knife, shave the corn kernels into a bowl. Discard the corncob.

To serve, melt 2 tablespoons of butter in a skillet or sauté pan. Heat the crawfish tail meat pieces and corn in the butter. Using small shot glasses, sake cups or demitasse cups, place a few warmed pieces of crawfish in each cup. Fill the cups with the hot shooter broth. Garnish the shots with corn kernels and chive sticks.

ALMOND SHRIMP

SERVES: 36 bites, 12 as appetizers or 6 as entrées

36	Louisiana shrimp, large to jumbo size, raw peeled with tails left on		1 pound	self-rising flour seasoned with salt and pepper
1/2 gallon	peanut oil		8 ounces	sweet chile glaze*
2 quarts	buttermilk, Bulgarian style, full fat		8 ounces	Zea Sweet Stir-fry Spicy Garlic Soy Sauce*

SLAW

4	whole carrots, peeled and cut into matchstick-size pieces 2 to 3 inches long (julienned)		4 cups	fresh cabbage strips, cut into matchstick-size pieces 2 to 3 inches long (julienned)

DIRECTIONS

Slice or julienne the carrots and cabbage by cutting into matchstick size pieces two to three inches long and toss together for a colorful bed of fresh flavors.

GARNISH

1 bunch	fresh basil leaves cut in thin strips (chiffonade)		1 bunch	green onions, sliced on diagonal
1 bunch	fresh cilantro leaves		1 cup	sliced almonds, toasted

DIRECTIONS

Shell and butterfly the shrimp, leaving the tails on. Devein them by running a paring knife down the back of the shrimp, cutting about 1/4 inch deep so the shrimp spreads open.

Using two large rectangular or oval roasting pans, each 2 to 3 inches deep, pour the buttermilk into one and the seasoned flour into the other.

This three-step breading process provides a full crunchy coating: Dip a shrimp completely into the flour and shake it until only a light dusting of flour has adhered to the shrimp. Dip into the buttermilk, coating the shrimp completely. Dip the shrimp back into the flour, coating it completely and heavily. Repeat the procedure on each shrimp until each is breaded.

Pour peanut oil into the electric deep fryer or skillet and heat to 350°F, checking the temperature with the thermometer. Add shrimp a few at a time so they are not touching and fry until golden. Remove them with a slotted spoon and drain them on paper towels. On each serving plate, create a bed with the cabbage-and-carrot slaw. Place the shrimp on the bed of slaw, either standing them on end, tail up, or laying them on their sides. Drizzle equal amounts of the sweet chile glaze and the stir-fry spicy garlic soy sauce onto each shrimp. Garnish with almonds, cilantro, basil and green onions. If serving as a hors d'oeuvre or canapé, offer toothpicks.

The Taste Buds are a triple threat trio of chefs who have developed ground-breaking restaurants and recipes at Zea Rotisserie and the new Semolina's Bistro Italia. Chef Gary Darling, Chef Hans Limburg and Chef Greg Reggio are the creators of Semolina, their initial restaurant venture.

How much is there to say about three indentured chefs who were hanging out on a beach in Hawaii, cooking for a celebrity event, and said the heck with working back home in the corporate kitchen. "We're serfs," said Gary. "No, we're surfing," corrected Greg. "That's the point," explained Hans. "Enough suits in our lives. We quit," they agreed.

They named themselves the Taste Buds, and the trio went on to max out their credit cards and wield a hammer. That was while they were testing new dishes in their kitchens at home.

They created Semolina, which took off like crazy. Semolina became so popular that the restaurant grew to several locations. Then they created Zea Rotisserie, another exciting restaurant that continues to expand.

Now Semolina has evolved to embrace Semolina's Bistro Italia, incorporating Mediterranean style dishes and other culinary escapades. None of the Taste Buds wear suits to work.

*Note: Any good-quality stir-fry spicy garlic soy sauce may be used. The sweet chile glaze and other brands of stir-fry spicy garlic soy sauce are available in the Asian foods sections of most grocery stores and specialty markets. They also may be purchased at http://www.zearestaurants.com.

Note: Two pieces of equipment are needed to prepare the recipe. They are a Fry Daddy electric deep fryer (or any other electric deep fryer) or a deep skillet, and a frying thermometer that reads up to 350°F.

Café Adelaide was named in honor of the late Adelaide Brennan of the Commander's Palace branch of the Brennan restaurant clan. Sassy and sophisticated, she regularly held court at the family's restaurants, dazzling guests with her wit and whimsy during the 1950s and 1960s, a time when celebrating la joie de vivre *was a high art.*

The Swizzle Stick Bar is appropriately named for the sparkle she added to conversation and the art of imbibing.

Café Adelaide's menu offers Creole classics with a twist of Big Easy creativity under the direction of managing partners Ti Martin and Lally Brennan.

Ti and Lally recently authored In the Land of Cocktails: Recipes and Adventures from the Cocktail Chicks, *a collection of recipes for both libations and high spirits.*

CAFÉ ADELAIDE
Marinated Louisiana Shrimp
WITH CRUSHED OPAL BASIL VINAIGRETTE

SERVES: 16 bites or 4 appetizers

VINAIGRETTE

16	jumbo (20 to 24 per pound) Louisiana shrimp, boiled and shelled,* but with tail shells on	2 teaspoons	sugar-cane vinegar
		1 teaspoon	fresh lime juice
1 tablespoon	opal or green basil	1 cup	diced bell peppers (a mix of green, red and yellow or orange)
2	shallots, finely chopped		
1 teaspoon	Creole mustard	1/2 cup	olive oil

For instructions on boiling shrimp, see page 93. May be prepared one day in advance.

DIRECTIONS

Tear opal basil into small pieces by hand and drop into a large bowl. Add all remaining ingredients except shrimp. Whisk the vinaigrette quickly for 2 to 3 minutes until well blended. Add shrimp to the vinaigrette, cover and refrigerate for at least 1 hour.

BEAN SALAD

1/2 cup	summer beans or peas (snap peas, snow peas, French beans)	1/2 bunch	fresh basil leaves, cut into thin strips (chiffonade)
1 medium	red onion, julienned	4 tablespoons	sugar-cane vinegar
16	cherry tomatoes, halved	3 tablespoons	olive oil
			kosher or sea salt to taste
			black pepper to taste

DIRECTIONS

To blanch the beans you'll need a large pot of boiling water and a sieve or fine strainer that fits into the pot. You will also need enough iced water to "shock" the beans after they're blanched.

Set the beans aside and combine all other ingredients in a large bowl. Place the beans in a sieve or large strainer and blanch them by plunging them into about a half-gallon of boiling water for about 15 seconds.

Take the beans in the sieve to a sink and allow them drain for a few seconds. Immediately drop the beans into iced water and allow them to drain well.

Toss the beans with the remaining ingredients.

Season the salad to taste with salt and pepper. To serve, divide the salad among plates or large platter and garnish with the marinated shrimp.

HERBSAINT
SHRIMP AND GRITS
WITH TASSO AND OKRA GRAVY

A surprising balancing act of flavors bring shrimp, sauce, and a grits cake into perfect harmony.

SERVES: 6 appetizers

TASSO AND OKRA GRAVY

18	fresh raw jumbo Louisiana shrimp (20 to 24 per pound), shelled and deveined		1/2 teaspoon	white pepper
			1/4 teaspoon	cayenne pepper
			1	bay leaf
10 tablespoons	unsalted butter		2 tablespoons	all-purpose flour
1 cup	diced onion		1 cup	shrimp stock*
1/2 cup	diced celery		1/4 cup	sautéed okra (1 cup raw)
1/2 cup	diced tasso		1/2 bunch	flat-leaf (Italian) parsley or chives for garnish
1 tablespoon	kosher or sea salt			

*For a shrimp-stock recipe, see page 93.

DIRECTIONS

In a 2-quart saucepan, over medium heat, melt 2 tablespoons of the butter and add the onion, celery, tasso, and spices. Let simmer for 5 to 7 minutes until soft. Add another 2 tablespoons of butter and allow it to melt into the vegetables. Create a roux by stirring the flour in with the vegetables to combine everything, about 5 minutes. Add shrimp stock and simmer on low for about 10 minutes. Set aside. (Whenever making a sauce that has some sort of roux in the base, always add the liquid in stages to prevent the sauce from becoming too thin. Thinning a sauce is always easier than thickening one).

Sauté the 18 shrimp in 6 tablespoons of butter until cooked through, about 6 to 10 minutes. Add the sauce to the pan and simmer together for about 2 minutes.

GRITS CAKES

1	jalapeño pepper, seeded and finely chopped	1/2 cup	Parmigiano-Reggiano cheese, finely grated
		3 cups	prepared grits

DIRECTIONS

Prepare the grits according to package directions and stir in the jalapeño pepper and Parmigiano-Reggiano cheese. Grease a rimmed sheet pan measuring 10 by 15 inches and at least 1 inch deep. Pour the cooked grits mixture into the pan and spread it evenly. Cover and refrigerate the pan of grits until it sets, approximately 1 hour. This may be done a day in advance and allowed to set overnight.

Preheat the oven to 350°F.

Bake the grits in the pan until they are hot and crisp on the bottom, about 20 minutes. Using a wet knife cut the grits into 3-inch squares. To serve, ladle about a tablespoon of sauce over each square of grits. Add three shrimp to each and garnish with parsley or chives.

Chef Donald Link drives the concept behind Herbsaint, a small bistro serving big flavors born of his Louisiana heritage. He is opinionated about some things — most things in fact, but especially grits. Grits are the Southern version of polenta and have the same benefits, one being that they can be cooled down and shaped for different preparations like this recipe.

"I will never cease to be amazed," Donald says, "that no matter where I get grits around the country at breakfast joints, I have never detected a smidgeon of salt in any of them. I'm amazed at how little effort some cooks spend on grits. I don't even really care what kind of grits they are as long as I get to eat them.

"Don't get me wrong though," he adds, "some grits are absolutely better than others. I may eat quick grits for a quick breakfast, but when I really want good grits I use John Taylor's Hoppin' John grits. They are coarse ground and need to be cooked much slower than your normal variety of grits."

Chef Donald is a James Beard Foundation honoree as Best Chef in the Southeast and can be found in the Herbsaint kitchen, unless he is over at Cochon, his other restaurant.

Michael Terranova

Al Copeland was a rock 'n 'roll kinda guy, New Orleans' own Elvis, with a personality to match, and a home-town hero to many. He had a taste for spice (he created Popeyes Fried Chicken) and speed (his collection of boats and cars was worth a king's ransom). And his exploits, in business and otherwise, often made front-page news.

Popeyes, Copeland's and Copeland's Cheesecake Bistro were only a few of his creations. They provided the foundation for an empire of food-related enterprises. He was obsessively secretive about his fried-chicken spice recipe, having discovered the power of distinctive flavor, and once he'd made his fortune with it, discovered that secrets had a value

Copeland's street smarts paid off when he swaggered down Wall Street; battled it out with the bankers and won in the end. Not bad for a scrappy kid from the housing projects. Not bad for anyone. He fought for the right to create his spectacular Christmas lights display at his home. He and novelist Anne Rice, another native New Orleanian, mixed it up over the décor of one of his restaurants. Rice called it gaudy. Copeland answered, "It's a matter of taste. Mine." His middle initial "C" could have stood for "controversial."

When he departed this earth, at a fairly early age, the ceremonies were typically Al. His fleets of cars, boats and trucks were put on display around his family mausoleum. The services started 15 minutes late, in his honor. He was carried to rest by a horse-drawn, antique glass hearse led by a jazz band. Once the sun went down, twinkling lights brightened the cemetery, just as they had at Al Copeland's home during the Christmas season.

AL COPELAND
BOILED SHRIMP
WITH WHITE REMOULADE SAUCE

This would not be a New Orleans appetizer cookbook without a shrimp remoulade recipe. New Orleans' fabled remoulade sauce originally was brick-red, thanks to the paprika and cayenne pepper content. Al Copeland, Jr., CEO of Al Copeland Investments, provided this recipe for a white remoulade sauce — a sparkling twist to an old favorite, and the only Copeland recipe ever published.

SERVES: 48 bites or 8 appetizers
BOILED SHRIMP

2 pounds	medium (21 to 25 to the pound) fresh raw Louisiana shrimp, in shells	2 quarts	water
1 packet	dry Zatarain's Crab & Shrimp Boil (or 1 tablespoon liquid Zatarain's Crab & Shrimp Boil)	2 quarts	ice cubes

DIRECTIONS

Place the dry or liquid seasoning in a large pot of water and bring to a boil. Add shrimp and return to a boil. Set a timer for 2 minutes then remove the pot from heat. Add the ice to the pot and stir thoroughly. Let the shrimp stand in the water and seasonings for 1/2 hour. Drain, shell and devein the shrimp. If they are to be served as finger food, leave the shrimp tails on. If serving as an appetizer, remove the tails. Set the shrimp aside to make the remoulade sauce.

YIELD: about 2 cups
WHITE REMOULADE SAUCE

1/4 cup	sour cream	1/4 teaspoon	cayenne pepper
1/2 cup	Creole mustard	1 tablespoon	worcestershire sauce
2 tablespoons	prepared horseradish	1 tablespoon	fresh-squeezed lemon juice
1/2 teaspoon	garlic powder	1/4 cup	minced curly parsley
1/2 teaspoon	freshly ground black pepper	1/4 cup	finely minced celery
1 tablespoon	twice-blanched and minced garlic	1 cup	mayonnaise
			additional parsley, for garnish

Place all ingredients except the mayonnaise and parsley garnish into a stainless steel mixing bowl and combine well with a wire whip. Add the mayonnaise gradually and combine well again.

ASSEMBLY

the reserved 2 pounds of cooked and shelled shrimp	lemon wedges for garnish
the reserved remoulade sauce	2 cups shredded lettuce

Assemble the dish by placing a bed of shredded lettuce in the center of the serving platter, or individual appetizer plates. Add the shrimp, with the tail ends arranged in the same direction and ladle a strip or dollop of remoulade sauce over each serving. Sprinkle with chopped parsley. Serve with a lemon wedge as garnish.

COMMANDER'S PALACE
SHRIMP AND TASSO HENICAN
FIVE-PEPPER JELLY & HOT-SAUCE BEURRE BLANC

The five-pepper jelly is a colorful accompaniment to almost any seafood or meat. The Crystal hot sauce beurre blanc is also versatile for other dishes.

SERVES: 36 bites

CRYSTAL HOT SAUCE BEURRE BLANC

pinch	garlic, very finely chopped	1/4 cup	heavy cream
pinch	French shallot, finely chopped	1-1/2 pounds	unsalted butter, softened
1/2 cup	Crystal hot sauce		

DIRECTIONS

Sauté garlic and shallots with one tablespoon of butter in a small saucepan until translucent. Add the Crystal hot sauce and reduce by 3/4. Add the heavy cream and reduce again by half. Slowly whip the softened butter into the reduced hot sauce mixture. Set aside.

SHRIMP

36	raw Louisiana jumbo (20 to 24 per pound) shrimp, shelled and deveined	36	pickled okra pods
3/4 cup	tasso in a one-inch matchsticks (julienne)	1	Five-Pepper Jelly recipe
1 cup	seasoned flour*	1	Crystal hot sauce beurre blanc recipe
1-1/2 cups	peanut or other vegetable oil	36	or more toothpicks

*See page 92 for seasoned-flour recipe.

DIRECTIONS

Make a 1/4-inch cut on the back of each shrimp and place one strip of tasso in the opening. Secure each strip of tasso with a toothpick. Coat each shrimp with the seasoned flour, and lightly shake to remove excess.

In a medium skillet, heat oil over high heat. (There should be enough oil to cover the shrimp). Fry shrimp until golden. Remove cooked shrimp and drain them on a paper towel to remove excess oil.

Place cooked shrimp in the Crystal hot sauce beurre blanc and toss until well coated.

Spread the five-pepper jelly onto a small serving dish or platter and alternately place shrimp and pickled okra on the jelly. Garnish with fresh herbs, such as parsley or dill, if desired.

Flagship of the Commander's Palace family of restaurants, managing partners Ti Martin and Lally Brennan keep the ambiance bright and flavors sparkling by using Creole ingenuity, commitment and a rich heritage of culinary expertise from the infamous Brennan restaurant clan.

Shrimp Henican was named for Joseph Henican, a long-time family friend, because Ti and Lally thought it would be amusing to name a shrimp dish after a gentleman who stands well over six feet tall.

5 PEPPER JELLY

6 ounces	Karo Light corn syrup
6 ounces	white vinegar
1	red bell pepper, finely diced
1	yellow bell pepper, finely diced
1	green bell pepper, finely diced
1/4 teaspoon	red pepper flakes
	kosher or sea salt, to taste

DIRECTIONS

In a small saucepan, reduce corn syrup and vinegar over medium heat until it's sticky and completely coats a spoon. Add remaining ingredients and cook until the peppers are soft. Add salt to taste. Set aside.

France and Spain were fundamental influences of Louisiana cooking. Cuvée draws from the past and updates it to the present with regional ingredients. The impressive wine list balances a contemporary Creole menu with finesse, as their name indicates.

YIELDS: 3 cups

WHITE REMOULADE SAUCE

1 cup	mayonnaise
1/2 cup	sour cream
1/4 cup	Creole mustard
3 teaspoons	horseradish, freshly grated or prepared
1/4 bunch	green onions, chopped
3 teaspoons	worcestershire sauce
1 teaspoon	Tabasco sauce
1/8 cup	heavy cream
1 tablespoon	sugar
1/2 teaspoon	minced garlic
1/4 cup	ketchup
1	hard boiled egg, chopped
	kosher or sea salt, to taste
	freshly ground black pepper, to taste
	cayenne pepper, to taste

Thoroughly mix all ingredients except salt and the two peppers. Once they are well combined, season with the salt and two peppers to taste.

CUVÉE
SHRIMP NAPOLEON
WITH REMOULADE SAUCE

Cuvée's shrimp Napoleon with white rather than red remoulade sauce is a signature dish, layering crisp merliton rounds with boiled shrimp and remoulade sauce and topped with a confetti array of colored bell peppers chives and endive.

SERVES: 12 Napoleons

SHRIMP NAPOLEON

3 pounds	shrimp, 36/40, peeled and deveined	3	eggs
3 gallons	water	2 quarts	vegetable or corn oil
1/2 cup	Zatarain's crab and shrimp boil	3 cups	Remoulade sauce
4	mirliton	2 cups	Cayenne beurre blanc sauce*
1 quart	all purpose flour		red and yellow bell peppers, thin julienne, 1 inch long (Garnish)
1/4 cup	Creole seasoning, Tony Chachere's		chives, chopped (Garnish)
1 quart	whole milk		Belgian endive, cleaned and cut using mostly white leaf (garnish)

See page 93 for beurre blanc sauce.

DIRECTIONS

Over high heat, in a large stock pot, bring the water and the seasoning to a boil. Add the shrimp, and cook until tender, approximately 4-minutes. When cooked, strain the shrimp, and place them on a baking sheet, in a single layer. Place the baking sheet in the refrigerator, and allow to cool. When the shrimp are cool, slice them in half lengthwise. Set aside.

In a large frying pot, heat the oil over high heat to 350°F. Slice the mirliton into 1/8-inch strips. You should get about 10 slices per mirliton. In a large mixing bowl, mix the flour and the Creole seasoning together thoroughly. In a separate medium mixing bowl, whisk the eggs and milk together until well combined to form an egg wash.

Dredge each mirliton chip in the flour mix then the eggwash mix then back into the flour mix. Place the chips carefully in the hot oil, and fry until golden brown on both sides. Make sure to flip the chips while in the oil to ensure even cooking. After each chip is cooked, remove them from the oil with a slotted spoon, and place the chips on a bed of paper towels. This will soak up the excess oil from the chips.

To serve, toss the cooked shrimp with the remoulade sauce. On each small appetizer plate, drizzle about a 1/2-ounce of cayenne beurre blanc sauce on the center of the plate. Place a mirliton chip on top of the beurre blanc, and top with a tablespoon of the shrimp remoulade, 2 to 3 shrimp. Repeat the chip and remoulade process twice. This will yield three layers of chips and shrimp remoulade, and finish with shrimp remoulade on top of the napoleon. Place a pinch of Belgian endive on top of the napoleon, followed by pepper curls, and a sprinkle of chopped chives.

P&J OYSTER COMPANY
OYSTERS BIENVILLE

SERVES: 48 bites or 8 appetizers

1 tablespoon	vegetable oil	6 tablespoons	grated Romano cheese
2/3 cup	finely chopped white mushrooms	4 tablespoons	dry bread crumbs
4 tablespoons	unsalted butter	1/4 cup	finely chopped Italian (flat-leaf) parsley
1 1/2 teaspoons	very finely chopped garlic	1 teaspoon	kosher or sea salt
4 large	French shallots, finely chopped		freshly ground black pepper
1/2 pound	fresh Louisiana shrimp, cooked, shelled and finely diced	1/2 teaspoon	cayenne pepper
1 tablespoon	all-purpose flour	2 dozen	plump and salty raw Louisiana oysters, freshly shucked the "liquor" from the shucked oysters
1/2 cup	brandy		
1/2 cup	heavy cream		
1 teaspoon	freshly ground white pepper	48	bite-size puff pastry shells or 8 tart-size pastry shells

DIRECTIONS

In a large, heavy saucepan, heat the vegetable oil over high heat and sauté the chopped mushrooms for about 4 minutes, stirring. Remove from the pan with a slotted spoon and press with another spoon to remove excess liquid and set aside. In the same pan, melt the butter over low heat and sauté the garlic and shallots for about 3 minutes, stirring frequently, until softened. Add the diced shrimp and stir to mix, then sprinkle evenly with the flour. Stir together, add the reserved mushrooms and increase heat to medium.

Stirring constantly, deglaze the pan with the brandy. Stir in the cream and cook for 2 to 3 minutes, until smooth. Stir in the Romano, dry bread crumbs, parsley, salt, a touch of black pepper and the cayenne to a soft, moundable consistency. A small amount of milk may be added if the mixture is too thick. Remove the pan from the heat and transfer the mixture to a glass or ceramic bowl. Cool to room temperature, then refrigerate for about 1 1/2 hours, or until thoroughly chilled.

Preheat the oven to 400°F.

Place the raw oysters in a large saucepan or deep skillet and top with the oyster liquor, adding white wine as necessary to cover them completely. Simmer on medium heat for 2 to 3 minutes until the edges curl.

If using the bite-size pastry shells, drain, cool and cut the oysters in half. If using the tart-size shells, use the oyster whole. Divide the oysters into the pastry shells and top with a generous scoop of Bienville sauce. Bake for 15 to 18 minutes, until nicely browned. Add a sprinkle of chopped chives or parsley for garnish if desired.

Arrange on serving platters or appetizer plates and serve immediately.

Arnaud's original oysters Bienville take their name from the restaurant's location on the Rue Bienville, which in turn was named for the founder of New Orleans, Jean Baptiste le Moyne, Sieur de Bienville, who became governor of the original French colony. As the story goes, the dish was created as a competitive response to the great attention oysters Rockefeller were attracting at Antoine's a few blocks away.

P&J Oysters, believed to be the country's oldest oyster shucking company, probably provided the oysters to Arnaud's as well as Antoine's when these recipes were first devised.

Arnaud's continues to use only P&J's fresh, raw oysters, both shucked and whole in the shell.

Restaurants in New Orleans observe great loyalty to their purveyors, especially ones that have supplied them with excellent products for decades. Chef Leah Chase says that, in 65 years of cooking at Dooky Chase's restaurant, she has never used an oyster from a supplier other than P&J.

Galatoire's 100-year celebration in 2005 was memorialized with a brass 100 on their front door handle.

The restaurant is one of New Orleans grand old gals, still flirtatious and coy, and now renewed and refreshed after a major renovation. (A facelift does wonders for the ego.)

Following tradition, reservations are accepted only for tables in the upstairs dining rooms. Downstairs, the prized seats are up for grabs by locals and visitors to the city, and many people good-naturedly stand in line for these seats, or pay someone to stand for them. It's worth the wait, since the veteran waiters know many of the regular customers' preferences for cocktails and dishes. This is but one of Galatoire's many idiosyncrasies.

Eccentric? Certainly. Any 100-year-old lady should be allowed to have her way.

YIELD: 1/2 cup

MEUNIÈRE BUTTER

1 stick (8 tablespoons)	salted butter
1 tablespoon	chopped parsley

In a medium sauté pan over medium heat, place the butter in pan and melt until a foam appears about 3 to 4 minutes. Once foam has appeared, add parsley and cook for 1 more minute, or when the butter starts to brown. Once that happens, remove from heat and serve.

OYSTERS EN BROCHETTES

Crisp and on the outside and bursting with flavor inside, oysters en brochettes (French for "on skewers") are a perennial favorite at Galatoire's. Bacon flavors seep into the oysters during the frying process for a sweet, smoky taste. You will require wooden skewers for this recipe. Trim them to the length needed to fit in your electric fryer or frying pan. The skewers should be of a sufficient length to hold one oyster and one piece of bacon or three oysters and three pieces of bacon.

SERVES: 36 bites or 6 appetizers

1 gallon	vegetable oil		2 cups	whole milk
18	thick slices smoked bacon,		2 cups	all-purpose flour
	cut in half to produce 36 pieces		1 recipe	meunière butter
36	large raw Louisiana oysters,			toast points, for garnish
	shucked			lemon wedges, for garnish
2	large eggs			wooden skewers for serving

DIRECTIONS

Heat the oil to 350°F in a large sauté pan or fryer, taking care to maintain the temperature. In a separate, medium-size sauté pan, cook the bacon over medium heat for 3 to 4 minutes to render some of the fat from the meat. The bacon should be only lightly browned, and still pliable enough to fold for skewering. Drain on paper towels.

Skewer one oyster with one piece of bacon, folding the bacon to the proper size. Repeat the process for each skewer, alternating the oyster and the bacon. Set the skewered oysters and bacon aside.

In a medium-size bowl, whisk together the eggs and milk to create an egg wash. Place the flour in a shallow baking pan. First dip the skewered oysters and bacon into the egg wash, allowing the excess liquid to drip off. Then coat the oysters and bacon thickly with the flour before shaking off the excess flour.

Place the skewers in the hot oil and fry them for 4 to 5 minutes, until they are golden and float to the top. Be careful not to overcook the oysters. Remove each skewer from the oil to a plate lined with paper towels.

Place the skewers at the center of the platter or appetizer plates. Remove the oysters and bacon pieces from the skewer by holding one end of it to slide them off. Nap the meunière butter over the top of the oysters, allowing the sauce to pool slightly at the bottom of the plate. Garnish each dish with toast points and a lemon wedge.

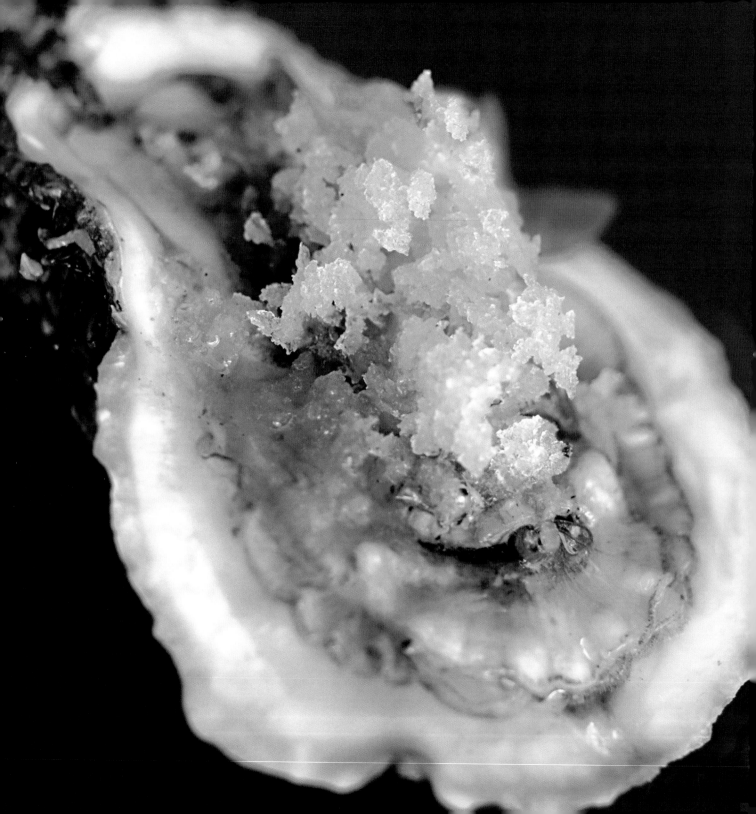

CHEF ROBERT BARKER
OYSTERS CAMILLE

Raw oysters are terrific, and the colder they are the better. In this dish, they're topped with a tiny snowball of spicy, pinkish cocktail sauce that's made with fresh tomato juice and seasonings. When the oyster and the frosty ice reach the palate, they burst with flavor. The combination of savory ice and briny oyster is a revelation. To achieve the optimum level of chilled thrill, everything used in serving Oysters Camille should be cold, even the plates and forks.

SERVES: 4 as appetizers and 8 as hors d'oeuvres

24	oysters, well chilled	1 tablespoon	chopped parsley or
24	oyster bottom shells		green onion for garnish

TOMATO GRANITA

8 large	Roma tomatoes, roughly chopped		Tabasco or other hot pepper sauce, to taste
1 teaspoon	worcestershire sauce		kosher or sea salt, to taste
1 large	lemon, juiced		crushed ice

DIRECTIONS

In a food processor purée the tomatoes until smooth.

Line a strainer with a paper coffee filter or cheesecloth and rest the strainer over a medium-size bowl. Pour the purée into the lined strainer and allow the water from the purée to drip into the bowl and produce a pinkish, watery liquid. With your fingers, gently press down on the purée to release as much tomato water as possible. The total yield should be about 1 cup of liquid. Set aside.

After discarding the paper filter or cheesecloth with the drained purée, add the remaining ingredients to the tomato water. Pour the mixture into a shallow, covered sheetpan and freeze overnight.

HORSERADISH MIGNONETTE

2 tablespoons	freshly grated or prepared horseradish	3 tablespoons	olive oil
1	shallot, finely diced	1/4 cup	champagne vinegar
1 teaspoon	freshly cracked black pepper		kosher or sea salt, to taste
			chopped parsley, for garnish

DIRECTIONS

In a separate bowl, whisk together all of the mignonette ingredients and season to taste.

To serve, shuck the oysters and place them in their bottom shells on a bed of crushed ice. Remove the frozen granita from the freezer and rake it with a fork until it reaches a fine, snowball-like consistency.

On each oyster place 1 tablespoon of the horseradish mignonette, then top it with 1 tablespoon of the tomato granita. Garnish with chopped parsley or green onion.

One of the privileges of being a chef, or a proprietor, is the ability to name a dish as they choose.

At our family home for Thanksgiving, the kids are assigned KP duty, and Robert prepares Thanksgiving dinner. His daughter, Camille, is now almost old enough to join that brigade, especially since she's made many television cooking show appearances assisting her father. It is time for her to learn that with fame comes hard work.

I taught Chef Robert how to peel potatoes. Many years later, in appreciation, he taught me how to make this magnificent appetizer.

After attending a culinary school in New Orleans Robert apprenticed at Arnaud's Restaurant in New Orleans, then worked with Chef Wolfgang Puck in California. He returned to New Orleans as Chef Emeril Lagasse's executive sous-chef at Emeril's New Orleans flagship restaurant, then moved on to earn his own executive chef's toque, which he usually replaces with a baseball cap.

These days, at Thanksgiving time, he does the shopping and orders us around while he presides over the turkey roasting and duck smoking, then later prepares a wonderful gumbo with the leftovers. We try to help. We are, he says, not quite as adept as his professional kitchen crew, but we are family, and we're happy to work for food.

At one time Kevin Vizard was New Orleans' peripatetic chef, launching new restaurants or cooking in high profile establishments.

Following tours of duty at Commander's Palace and Café Adelaide, as well as stints at Mr. B's, and several other establishments, Chef Kevin, a lifelong New Orleanian, has unveiled his latest venture in a cozy, vine-covered building uptown.

His followers get a kick out of chasing him, betting on who can find Kevin first. He continuously reinvents himself and his witty recipes, drawing on classical flavors and contemporary thinking.

Vizard's has emerged once again as an Uptown favorite in a new guise on Magazine Street with his wife and business partner, Cammie. The place is a virtual clubhouse for Uptowners looking for approachable food with strong New Orleans connections and a dose or two of creativity.

VIZARD'S
CARPETBAGGER OYSTER FILET

YIELD: 36 bites or 12 appetizers

1	beef tenderloin, about 1 pound, semi-frozen		juice of 1/2 lemon
	kosher or sea salt, to taste	1	bay leaf
	freshly ground black pepper, to taste	1 tablespoon	finely minced French shallot
36	raw shucked Louisiana oysters	1/2 cup	dry red wine
1 cup	oyster liquor	1/2 teaspoon	chopped fresh thyme
1 cup	olive oil	1 tablespoon	unsalted butter
1 tablespoon	garlic, chopped	1/2 cup	demi-glace
		1/2 pound	Brie cheese, cut into 1-inch by 1/8-inch squares

SAUCE DIRECTIONS

Preheat the oven to 350°F.

In a small sauté pan, over medium heat, sauté 1/2 of the garlic and the minced shallot for 2 minutes, until slightly transparent. Add the red wine and deglaze the pan by increasing the heat to bring the liquid to a quick boil, while stirring to loosen and partially dissolve the garlic bits. The deglazing process should take approximately 2 minutes. Once the pan is deglazed, add 1/2 of the oyster liquor and the thyme to the liquid and simmer until it is reduced to 2/3 of the original amount. Add the demi-glace and reduce again to 2/3 of the original amount. Stir in the butter until all of it is melted.

Place the saucepan over low heat and cover for later use. Stir the sauce occasionally to prevent a film from forming on top of the sauce.

BEEF SLICES AND OYSTERS DIRECTIONS

Preheat the broiler to a high heat.

Slice semi-frozen raw beef tenderloin into 36 slices, each 1/8 inch thick. Season with salt and pepper, to taste. Set the slices aside. In a large saucepan combine the remaining 1/2 cup of oyster liquor, all of the olive oil, lemon juice and bay leaf, and the remaining 1/2 tablespoon chopped garlic. Drop in the oysters and poach them for 1 to 2 minutes, until the edges begin to curl.

Drain the oysters and set them aside. Discard the poaching liquid.

Wrap a slice of beef tenderloin around each oyster and pierce each with a toothpick for easy serving. Place the skewered oysters and beef slices under the broiler for 6 minutes, or until brown. When they are done remove them from the broiler.

Place a square of Brie on each plate. Warm the plates in the oven to soften the cheese, about 30 seconds. As the plates are removed from the warming oven, place a piece of skewered oyster and beef on each square of Brie and drizzle some of the sauce onto each. Serve immediately.

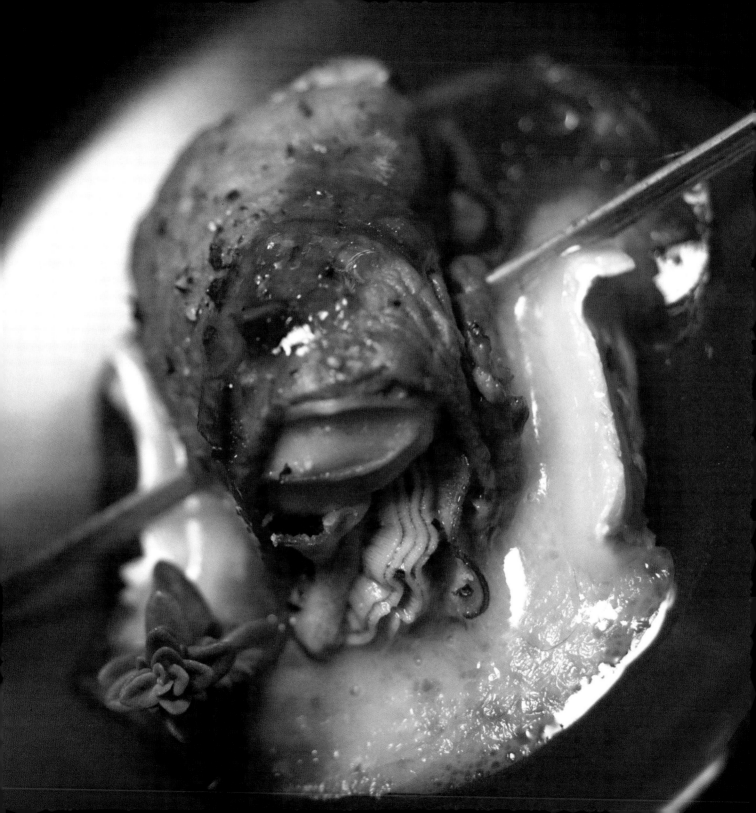

Poached Oysters and Pasta

IN WHITE-WINE GARLIC CREAM

Placed in individual sushi plates, this recipe makes entertaining bites. Served in larger dishes, it is a spectacular appetizer or even entrée.

SERVES: 40 bites, 12 appetizers or 4 entrées

4 teaspoons	butter			free of shell pieces
4 teaspoons	minced French shallot		1 teaspoon	pastis or other anise-flavored liqueur,
3 teaspoons	chopped garlic			such as Herbsaint or Pernod
8 tablespoons	chopped parsley			kosher or sea salt, to taste
1 cup	dry white wine			white pepper, to taste
2 cups	heavy whipping cream		3 cups	angel hair pasta, cooked
1/4 cup	strained raw Louisiana			sprigs of parsley, for garnish
	oyster liquor			grated Parmigiano-Reggiano cheese,
40	shucked oysters,			to taste, for garnish

DIRECTIONS

In a 2-quart saucepan melt the butter over high heat and add the chopped shallot, garlic and parsley. Reduce the heat to medium-high, and sauté for 3 minutes, until transparent.

Add the wine to deglaze the pan. Allow the vegetables and wine to simmer, until the liquid is reduced to 2/3 of the original amount.

When the liquid is reduced, add the cream and bring to a boil. Add the raw oysters and the oyster liquor to the vegetables and wine reduction. Season the liquid with the anise liqueur, and the salt and pepper. Cook the oysters until the edges curl, approximately 2 1/2 to 3 minutes.

To serve, place the pasta in a bowl appropriate to your style of service and top with the oysters and the white-wine garlic cream. Garnish with parsley sprigs and grated Parmigiano-Reggiano cheese, to taste.

Chef Tom Wolfe keeps this beloved restaurant on the favorites list for French Quarter residents, who use it as their personal dining room. Chef Tom has always cooked but also graduated from Delgado's Culinary Arts program along with numerous other well-established chefs. Delgado seems to have graduated one serious class a few years back and they each seem to have come into their own.

His experience at Mr. B's and Emeril's grounded him in the flair and flavors that have kept New Orleans culinary ingenuity a touchstone of creativity. His work has resulted in national honors and accolades, and has kept him in the top tier of chef-owners.

The mural over the bar depicts City Park's peristyle, hence the name former chef-owner Anne Kearney Sand gave to the old Marti's restaurant on Rampart.

During Marti' Shambra's time, guests included Tennessee Williams. Author Marcelle Bienvenu recalled a time when she requested a Sazarac with a dozen oysters, then left the room. When she returned, he was sitting at her place, happily indulging in her dinner.

The waiter whispered that it was Mr. Tennessee, and he always got whatever he wanted. Her order was duplicated, quickly served, and both guests were satisfied. Marcelle said he never even looked up.

P&J OYSTER COMPANY
OYSTERS ROCKEFELLER

SERVES: 72 bites or 16 appetizers

2 tablespoons	unsalted butter	2 tablespoons	finely chopped Italian (flat-leaf) parsley
12 slices	raw bacon, very finely chopped	1/3 cup	Herbsaint or Pernod anisette liqueur
4 cups	finely chopped celery	1 tablespoon	finely chopped fresh basil
1 cup	finely chopped green bell pepper		kosher or sea salt, to taste
3 tablespoons	very finely chopped garlic		freshly ground black pepper, to taste
1 cup	finely chopped white onions	3 dozen	plump and salty raw Louisiana oysters, freshly shucked, with flat bottom shells reserved
4 cups	fresh spinach, blanched, drained and chopped		
2	bay leaves	72	bit-size puff pastry shells or 16 tart-size pastry shells
1 pinch	dried thyme		
1 pinch	cayenne pepper		

DIRECTIONS

In a medium-size sauté pan, melt the butter over medium heat and cook the bacon until the fat has been rendered and bacon is crisp, about 5 minutes. Add the celery, green pepper, garlic and onions, then sauté until the vegetables are softened, 4 to 5 minutes. Add the spinach and stir for 5 more minutes. Stir in the bay leaves, thyme, cayenne, and parsley, then drizzle in the Herbsaint or Pernod, and continue cooking for 1 minute.

Reduce heat and simmer for 2 more minutes. Remove the bay leaves, add the basil and season to taste with salt and pepper.

In a blender or food processor, purée the vegetable and liqueur mixture, in batches if necessary. Place the purée back into the original pan, mixing thoroughly. Transfer to a covered container, cool to room temperature and refrigerate for about 1 hour or until the mixture is firm.

Preheat the oven to 400°F.

Place the raw oysters in a large saucepan or deep skillet and top with the oyster liquor, adding white wine as necessary to cover them completely. Simmer on medium heat for 2 or 3 minutes, until the oysters' edges curl. If using the bite-size pastry shells, drain the oysters, cool them and cut them in half. If using the larger pastry shells, leave the oysters whole.

Divide the oysters into the pastry shells and top with a generous scoop of Rockefeller sauce. Add a sprinkle or shaving of Parmigiano-Reggiano cheese if desired. Bake for 15 to 18 minutes, until nicely browned.

Arrange the filled pastry shells on serving platters or appetizer plates and serve immediately.

DICKIE BRENNAN'S BOURBON HOUSE
OYSTER SHOOTERS

Refreshing, delicious and simple to knock back.

EACH RECIPE SERVES: 24 oyster shooters

OYSTER SHOOTERS IN CHAMPAGNE MIGNONETTE WITH CAVIAR

1/2 cup	champagne		kosher or sea salt and
1/4 cup	rice vinegar		freshly cracked black pepper
1/4 cup	minced French shallot	24	raw shucked Louisiana oysters
1 tablespoon	Creole mustard	6 ounces	choupique caviar
1 tablespoon	parsley		

DIRECTIONS

Whisk together all ingredients except olive oil, caviar and oysters. Slowly whisk in oil and season to taste. Place each raw oyster in a shot glass and top each with mignonette and a dollop of caviar.

OYSTER SHOOTERS WITH GRANITÉ

1 cup	dry white wine		freshly cracked black pepper, to taste
1 cup	satsuma juice*		fresh mint leaves, julienned, for garnish
	dash of lemon juice	24	raw shucked Louisiana oysters

Juices of other citrus, such as navel and blood oranges, can be substituted for satsuma.

DIRECTIONS

Combine all ingredients except oysters and mint, and freeze in a shallow pan.

Divide citrus segments and liquids among 24 shot glasses. Top each with a raw oyster and a teaspoon of granité. Garnish with julienned mint.

OYSTER SHOOTERS WITH CUCUMBER AND TOBIKO

1 cup	finely diced cucumber, seeds and skin removed	1/2 teaspoon	minced chives
1/2 cup	rice-wine vinegar	1/2 cup	wasabi tobiko
1/2 teaspoon	chile pepper flakes	3/4 cup	seaweed salad, for garnish
		24	raw shucked Louisiana oysters

DIRECTIONS

Place all ingredients except seaweed salad and oysters in a bowl, and mix.

Divide cucumber mixture among 24 shot glasses. Top each with a raw oyster and garnish with seaweed salad.

Dickie Brennan is another of New Orleans' leading restaurant entrepreneurs, delighting in the creation of new concepts and successfully establishing them in popular hot spots.

He's also a scion of the far-ranging Brennan family — the Commander's Palace group — and learned the business at his father Dick's side. When Dick Brennan was at Commander's he could make Friday afternoon at the restaurant a memorable experience.

Dickie Brennan's Bourbon House (fittingly situated on Bourbon Street), is seafood-focused. Dickie's vision also encompasses Dickie Brennan's Steak House and the Palace Cafe, each distinctive, with menus cast solidly in the New Orleans mold.

In his younger years he spent time in the kitchen of the famed Roger Vergé at the Moulin de Mougins on the French Riviera, broadening his culinary expertise, although now he spends a bit more time in his restaurants' dining rooms than in the kitchens. Those at the stoves, however, know to be alert.

Bayona is one of the reasons New Orleans attracts food lovers from around the world. Chef Susan Spicer and proprietor Regina Keever founded the restaurant in 1990. Its cool, lush patio is tucked behind a 200-year-old Creole cottage in the French Quarter on Dauphine Street, which carried the name Camino de Bayona during New Orleans' Spanish colonial period.

Susan's take on international cuisine is found in many of her favorite recipes, and her style is pure serendipity, with an occasional dash of Big Easy flavor. Among her prestigious professional honors is her selection by the James Beard Foundation in 1993 as Best Chef, Southeast.

She is a partner in Herbsaint, whose kitchen is heaed by Chef Donald Link, her friend and former executive sous-chef.

Susan's cookbook, Crescent City Cooking: Unforgettable Recipes from Susan Spicer's New Orleans, is an exciting, must-have addition to any kitchen bookshelf.

BAYONA
GROUPER CEVICHE
WITH GUACAMOLE

This combination of two Mexican classics is light and refreshing, just right for a cold starter. The guacamole can stand alone as another crowd-pleasing dip or an accompaniment to other offerings.

SERVES: 8 hors d'oeuvres or 4 as appetizer courses

CEVICHE

1 pound	fresh grouper fillet (red snapper or redfish may be substituted.)	1/2	medium red onion, very finely diced
4	medium limes, juiced	1	jalapeño, seeded and finely diced
1 teaspoon	kosher or sea salt		

DIRECTIONS

Dice fish into 1/4-inch pieces and place in a glass or stainless steel bowl. Add lime juice and salt and stir well. Let sit for 5 minutes.

Add onion and jalapeño and stir. Taste and adjust with more salt or lime juice, or more jalapeño if a spicier ceviche is preferred.

Ceviche can be prepared up to 1 hour before serving. Keep refrigerated until ready to serve.

GUACAMOLE

2	ripe Hass avocados, peeled, pitted and diced	1/2 teaspoon	minced garlic (optional)
1/2 bunch	scallions, finely sliced from white to green	2	medium limes, juiced kosher or sea salt to taste splash of hot sauce
1/2 bunch	cilantro leaves, roughly chopped	1 bag	tortilla chips for garnish

DIRECTIONS

Mix all ingredients in a small bowl. Taste and adjust seasonings as desired.

Guacamole can be prepared up to 30 minutes before serving.

Place ceviche in tall, martini-like glasses and top with guacamole. Serve with crisp corn tortilla chips, preferably home-made.

CHEF GREG REGGIO

REDFISH ON THE HALF SHELL
WITH DILL SAUCE

This method of preparing fish is also known as "fisherman-style." When the fish's bones are removed, the skin remains on one side of each of the two fillets. During grilling, the skin acts as a moisture retainer, keeping the flesh tender as it grills.

When the fillets are placed directly on the grill, skin side down, the skin hardens and chars. This allows the fish either to be served as a whole fillet on a serving board, ready to be sliced, or presented whole. The fish can be divided into beautiful slices or bites, leaving the skin behind for delightful appetizers slices drizzled with the dill sauce.

SERVES: 4

4	fresh redfish fillets, 6 to 7 ounces each and 1/2 to 3/4 inches thick, skin on	4 teaspoons	Chef Paul Prudhomme's Blackened Redfish-Magic Seasoning Blend or other preferred seasonings*
4 teaspoons	unsalted butter, melted and clarified		springs of fresh herbs, such as rosemary, thyme, basil or oregano, optional

See page 92 for blackened seasoning recipe.

NOTES:

Chef Greg doe not marinate his fillets, but a marinade does add flavor to the fish, both inside and outside. You may use your favorite marinade.

If you'd like to enhance the flavor of the smoke, place a couple of handfuls of fresh herb sprigs — such as rosemary, thyme, basil or oregano — below the cooler side of the grill surface and beneath the fish. Wood chips soaked in water serve the same purpose. A long fish spatula will be needed to properly remove the fillet from the grill.

If the cooked fillets have been refrigerated overnight, they will slice more cleanly, especially if done with a knife that has been dipped in water.

DIRECTIONS

Either build a bank of coals on one side of a coal-fired grill, or heat only one side of a gas grill. When the coals have burned down and are coated with ash, they should be ready.

Dust the skinless side of each fillet with 1 teaspoon of seasonings and place it directly on the cool side of the grill. Cover the grill and cook the fillets for 6 to 7 minutes. The fish will be done when the thickest part of the fillet is pressed with the tip of a finger and the impression remains. Alternately, gently flake the fish open; if the flesh is opaque, the fillet is done.

When the fillets are cooked, remove them from the grill and brush the skinless side of each one with clarified butter.

Redfish on the half shell is a wonderful appetizer for seafood lovers. It is simple to create a splendid, beautiful fillet that's spicy flavorful on the outside and tender on the inside. A lot like Greg's personality.

Greg is one of the Taste Buds, a triple threat trio of chefs who have developed ground-breaking restaurants and recipes at Zea Rotisserie, and the new Semolina's Bistro Italia. Chef Gary Darling and Chef Hans Limburg are his partners.

DILL SAUCE

2/3 cup	mayonnaise
2-3 tablespoons	minced fresh dill, or 1 tablespoon dried
1 tablespoon	white vinegar
1 tablespoon	Creole mustard
1/2 teaspoon	dehydrated onion flakes*
6 drops	Tabasco
2 tablespoons	freshly squeezed lemon juice

These can be found on the spice shelves of stores and markets.

DIRECTIONS

Combine all ingredients well and chill.

To serve, slice the fillets and arrange the slices on a serving platter or on individual small plates. Ladle some of the dill sauce on each slice and garner with fresh dill. The fillets also may be served whole, to allow portions of the fish to be removed from the hardened skin.

Lüke is Chef John Besh's version of an old New Orleans brasserie from the turn of the past century.

The menu's mainstays are fresh seafood, charcuterie and hearty dishes combining French and German Old World cooking.

Lüke's decor includes rattan bistro chairs, blackboard specials and newspaper racks. Focal points such as tin ceilings, an oyster bar and a glassed-in kitchen create a warm and casual ambiance.

An acclaimed chef and Louisiana native, John Besh also presides over Restaurant August, Besh Steak, and La Provence, keeping a full plate. He is a James Beard Foundation honoree as Best Chef, Southeast in 2006. His flagship, Restaurant August, has consistently been a showcase for the sophisticated side of his creativity. Lüke demonstrates his casual good taste and sense of humor. Besh's love of the outdoors, hunting, fishing, and bayous underscore his understanding of Louisiana's native cuisine.

LÜKE
SALMON AND CAVIAR BEGGAR'S PURSES

Beggar's purses are usually made from crispy dough stuffed with tidbits. This novel approach uses slices of smoked salmon filled with sour cream and tops the chive-tied bundles with Louisiana choupique caviar.

SERVES: 8 beggar's purses

PECAN CRUST

1	8-ounce package smoked salmon, sliced	1 bunch	fresh chives
1	8 ounce carton sour cream	1	small red onion, finely chopped
		1 ounce	Louisiana choupique caviar*

Salmon roe would be a good substitute for the choupique caviar.

DIRECTIONS

Place the bunch of fresh chives in a sieve. Dip the chives into a pot of boiling water for 15 seconds to blanch them. Remove the sieve and rinse the chives under cold water. They will retain their color and be more flexible to tie.

Separate the bunch of chives into two halves. Finely chop the chives in one half of the bunch and set aside the other half-bunch.

Combine the sour cream, finely chopped chives and onion in a medium bowl. Mix until well combined.

Remove the salmon from the packaging and separate the slices on a work surface. Place a dollop of the sour-cream mixture at the center of each salmon slice. Gather the edges of the slices from all sides and bring them upwards, creating a purse-like package. Using the remaining chives, tie each purse closed with one of the long whole chives.

To finish, place a small amount of caviar atop each purse. Garnish with a very small dollop of sour-cream mixture and a sprinkle of chopped chives.

GLENN VESH
Seared Tuna
with Mirliton Relish

SERVES: 24 pieces or 6 appetizers

1 pound	center-cut loin of raw tuna, best quality		2 tablespoons	aji-mirin (sweet rice wine for cooking)
2 tablespoons	blackened seasoning*		1/4 cup	wasabi aioli
1 tablespoon	vegetable oil		2 tablespoons	black or white sesame seeds
1	mirliton			

See page 92 for blackened seasoning recipe

DIRECTIONS

Lightly dust the tuna with the blackened seasoning. Gently shake off excess seasoning.

In a medium sauté pan over a very high flame, heat the vegetable oil. Place the tuna in the pan and sear each side for 10 seconds. Remove the tuna from heat and refrigerate to stop the cooking process, approximately 20 minutes.

Slice mirliton into long, thin strips, stopping on each side before reaching the seeds, then cut the long strips into pieces 2 to 3 inches long to yield a thin julienne. In a medium-size metal bowl, add mirliton and marinate with the aji-mirrin. Cover and refrigerate for 30 minutes.

Remove the seared tuna from the refrigerator and, using a very sharp knife, hold it flat and slice it into approximately 24 medallions 1/4-inch thick. Set aside.

If the tuna is to be served on a large platter, spread all the mirliton relish across the platter evenly. Then arrange the tuna medallions on the relish.

If the tuna is to be served on appetizer plates, place the relish, in dollops of about 2 ounces each, on each plate. Arrange about 4 tuna medallions over each mound of relish.

When using either serving method, top each tuna medallion with 1/2 teaspoon of wasabi aioli and sprinkle sesame seeds on each.

WASABI AIOLI

1	egg yolk		1/4 teaspoon	black pepper
4 ounces	wasabi paste		3/4 cup	canola oil
1 teaspoon	kosher salt		1/4 cup	olive oil

DIRECTIONS

Blend all ingredients together except the oil. Slowly pour both oils in a blender and blend well.

Glenn Vesh probably attends — or attends to — more parties than anyone in town. He's an entertaining secret resource and cooks like crazy.

Through his firm, appropriately named Perfect Presentations, he provides exuberant floral designs and décor for every kind of special occasion, from dressing the surroundings to having the tables arranged and properly set. When no one's watching, he'll even rearrange the furniture.

Outdoors, indoors, casual or formal, Glenn's flowers and décor are a marvelous backdrop for fine food, and can make a special event spectacular.

Nanci Easterling walked into a kitchen, felt the spirited magic, and has never left it. Her fascination with extraordinary food and service has driven her to the top of the catering business. Nanci's fastidious nature and international culinary exposure create a persnickety sensibility about what is right for certain events.

This security for experienced and inexperienced hostesses is invaluable. The real joy is in knowing that Nanci has taken over. Tables are draped, flowers appear, the music tunes up, beverages are served properly, and food is arrayed in all its colorful flavors.

Her events have ranged from the most elaborate possible to intimate dinner parties, picnics for road trips and corporate luncheons. Large and magnificently grand, or small and casual, it will be right, it will be delicious, and you'll never worry – just accept the accolades.

Easy elegance, as it should be.

FOOD ART

CARPACCIO OF BEEF

WITH THREE-PEPPER RELISH

Oriental spoons, which are widely available in specialty or gourmet shops, are perfect holders for almost any single serving of a bite. If Oriental spoons are not available, the teaspoons in your silver drawer will do just fine. Arrange them in pretty rows or circles on a tray or platter for easy serving.

SERVES: 20 bites

1 pound	raw beef tenderloin, preferably center-cut, about 3 inches thick, cleaned and frozen	1/4 cup	Parmigiano-Reggiano cheese, thinly shaved
1/2 cup	olive oil, flavored if desired		kosher or sea salt, to taste
1/3 cup	micro greens*		black pepper, to taste
1	small green bell pepper, finely diced		balsamic vinegar, to taste, optional
1	small yellow bell pepper, finely diced	20	ceramic oriental soup spoons,
1	small red bell pepper, finely diced		or substitute teaspoons

Micro greens are very young, tiny greens or herbs that are intensely flavored and beautiful.

DIRECTIONS

Cut the frozen tenderloin in paper-thin slices.* Cut each sliced round into a half circle. Lightly spray or brush the slices with olive oil and sprinkle with salt and pepper, as desired.

Place each of the seasoned tenderloin slices on a flat surface, and lay a pinch of the micro greens on top.

Loosely roll each slice of beef around the greens, allowing the greens to peek out for a nice color contrast. Place each beef carpaccio in the bowl of a spoon.

In a separate bowl, mix all the finely diced peppers together. Lightly sprinkle them over the beef carpaccios, and finish each spoon with a sprinkle of the shaved Parmigiano-Reggiano.

When ready to serve, drizzle with balsamic vinegar if desired. If not serving immediately, cover to preserve the color of the beef.

If unable to cut slices paper-thin, cut as thin as possible, then pound the slices with a kitchen mallet.

LA CÔTE BRASSERIE
SATSUMA-MARINATED DUCK
WITH MANGO RELISH AND SATSUMA VINAIGRETTE

Executive Chef Chuck prefers satsumas from the Becnel produce stand in Plaquemines Parish.

SERVES: 10 to 12 as appetizers

MARINATED DUCK BREASTS

2 pounds	duck breasts, each approximately 6 to 8 ounces	1 tablespoon	minced garlic
3	satsumas		freshly cracked black pepper, to taste

DIRECTIONS

Remove all silver skin from the duck breasts and trim some of the fat from them. Using a fine cheese grater, zest the satsumas. Reserve the leftover satsumas for the relish. Add the garlic and the pepper. Cover the duck breasts with the mixture and marinate for approximately 6 to 8 hours or overnight.

SATSUMA VINAIGRETTE

4	satsumas	1/4 teaspoon	finely minced garlic
1	French shallot, minced	1/2 cup	olive oil

DIRECTIONS

Remove the juice from the satsumas. In a small saucepan over medium heat, reduce the juice by half. Refrigerate the reduction until it is cold, for at least 1 hour.

After the reduced satsuma juice has cooled, combine it with chopped shallot, garlic and olive oil in a small mixing bowl. Whisk everything together and season with salt as needed.

PINEAPPLE-MANGO RELISH

1	fresh pineapple	1 tablespoon	chopped fresh cilantro
2	fresh mangoes	4 tablespoons	satsuma juice*, freshly squeezed
1	red onion, small dice		kosher or sea salt
2 tablespoons	chopped fresh basil		and freshly ground black pepper

Oranges, tangerines or other citrus fruits may be substituted if satsumas are not available.

DIRECTIONS

Peel the pineapple and slice the bottom off, enabling it to stand upright on its own. Cut the core from the pineapple and discard it. Peel the mangoes and cut them in half, exposing the pit. Remove the pit and discard.

Cut both the pineapple and mango pieces in a medium dice. In a large mixing bowl, combine the diced fruit with the onion, basil, cilantro and satsuma juice. Season to taste with salt and pepper. Cover and refrigerate.

La Côte Brasserie is located in an historic 1910 warehouse in the heart of the New Orleans Arts District. Executive Chef Chuck Subra, Jr., is a native Louisianian with a passion for creative Cajun cuisine, in keeping with the restaurant's impressive art collection.

FINAL PREPARATION

2 tablespoons	salad or vegetable oil

DIRECTIONS

Preheat oven to 350°F.

Heat the salad or vegetable oil in a sauté skillet on medium heat. Add the duck breasts and cook on both sides until golden brown. Place the duck breasts in a shallow pan into the preheated oven for approximately 4 minutes for medium-rare and 8 to 10 minutes for medium.

Remove from the oven and allow to rest 4 to 5 minutes.

To serve, place 2 ounces of the relish in the center of each plate. Slice the duck breast into approximately 1/4-inch medallions, yielding 10 to 12 slices. Place two or three medallions atop the relish on each plate and drizzle with 1 1/2 tablespoon of the satsuma vinaigrette.

GENE BOURG
LAMB LOLLIPOPS
WITH PECAN-MINT PESTO

Lamb is a dish appropriate to mention Gene Bourg. As a Times-Picayune writer and editor, Gene used to make reporters anxious then later restaurateurs tremble when he was the newspaper's restaurant critic.

Here Chef Leah Chase demonstrates exactly how much she feared his reviews. As the queen of Creole cuisine, she had nothing to worry about.

In fact, I was aware of several kitchens where his photograph was posted on the waiter's bulletin board. Not that it mattered. He was able to suss out the wary and the weak — both reporters, and chefs. Gene knows words and food — good, bad or indifferent, and is always forthright. If you agree or not with a critic is a matter of personal good taste.

That he is also a raconteur and a delightful guest is beside the point. At one memorable luncheon he appeared wearing New Orleans' summer uniform — a seersucker suit. That the other two gentlemen at the table were also wearing their seersucker suits made a picture that could only be seen here.

Following his retirement he has authored numerous articles for national food publications and books, and continues to offer his opinions. Critical, and otherwise.

For all of this, we thank him.

SERVES: 8 appetizers

PECAN-MINT PESTO

YIELDS: 1/2 cup

2 bunches	fresh mint	1/4 cup	extra-virgin olive oil
5 cloves	garlic	2 tablespoons	fresh-squeezed lemon juice
1/4 cup	pecans, whole or in pieces		kosher or sea salt, to taste
3 tablespoons	finely grated Parmigiano-Reggiano cheese		freshly ground black pepper, to taste

DIRECTIONS

Remove the mint leaves from the stems. Place the leaves, garlic and pecans into a food processor and pulse to yield a rough chop. In the same processor, add the Parmigiano-Reggiano cheese and the olive oil and blend until smooth. Add the lemon juice, and salt and pepper to taste. Set aside.

LAMB LOLLIPOPS

2	racks New Zealand lamb	1 bunch	fresh mint sprigs, for garnish
1/2 cup	pecan-mint pesto	1/4 cup	whole pecans, toasted, for garnish
2 tablespoons	vegetable oil		

DIRECTIONS

Preheat the oven to 400°F.

Pat the lamb racks dry with a clean towel to remove moisture. This will allow the pesto to adhere to the meat. Once the racks are dry, french each rib by cutting away the meat to expose the bone. Rub the meat generously with half of the prepared pecan-mint pesto.

In a medium sauté pan, over high heat, sear the racks of lamb. To do this, place the rack in the pan fat side down, for 2 to 3 minutes, until golden brown. Using the bones, turn the lamb on its side and sear each side of the rack for 2 to 3 minutes.

Place the seared lamb racks on a baking sheet in the preheated oven and cook for approximately 6 minutes for medium-rare, or longer if desired. Remove the racks from oven and allow them to cool slightly. Once they're cool enough to handle, using a sharp knife, slice between each bone to yield individual lamb chops.

To serve, create a bed of mint sprigs on the presentation plate. Place the individual lamb chops atop the mint sprigs. Add a 1/2 teaspoon of pesto on top of each lamb lollipop. To finish, sprinkle the toasted pecans on the plate as a garnish.

ASPARAGUS SPEARS
WITH PROSCIUTTO AND HERBED CHÈVRE

Prosciutto (a thin cured Italian ham) serves as a handy wrapper enclosing cheese and fresh asparagus. This technique may also be used to create numerous versions on the same theme. Consider American ham and cheddar cheese with fresh lettuce in the center as a bouquet. Also tempting would be thinly sliced roast beef with horseradish cream and blanched baby green beans. Poultry, such as sliced chicken or turkey with blanched sweet pea pods and whipped cream cheese, would also be colorful. A vegetarian version would replace the meat wrapper with lettuce, taking a page from the Asian play book.

These may be served either standing on end or lying basking on their side on a platter or tiny, individual serving plates.

SERVES: 24 pieces

1 bunch	asparagus, pencil size	1 tablespoon	balsamic vinegar
1/2 cup	goat cheese	12 slices	prosciutto
1 tablespoon	chopped fresh thyme	1 tablespoon	virgin olive oil
1/2 teaspoon	freshly ground black pepper		

DIRECTIONS

Cut the asparagus tops into 3-inch spears. Blanch them in boiling water for 30 seconds.

In a medium metal bowl, combine the goat cheese, thyme, pepper and balsamic vinegar, to yield an herbed goat-cheese spread.

Lay out the prosciutto slices and cut each in half vertically. Place 1 teaspoon of the goat cheese spread onto each prosciutto section.

Place three asparagus tips onto the goat cheese, leaving the tips exposed above the prosciutto. Wrap the prosciutto around the asparagus and the cheese spread. Cover and refrigerate.

To serve, stand bundles of asparagus spears on individual serving plates or a large platter. To finish, drizzle with olive oil.

In a city renowned for food and great restaurants, the Ritz-Carlton Hotel's executive chef Matt Murphy is the master of creations in Mèlange. He combines innate culinary sense and seasoned talent.

Chef Murphy trained at Commander's Palace under the late chef Jamie Shannon. Murphy has also worked in Michelin-starred restaurants throughout Europe and Asia.

He presides over a most unusual menu. The city's most heralded restaurants have come together to feature their most famous dishes in Mèlange, creating one extraordinary establishment.

Louisiana's flavors are highlighted in a menu that includes favorite local dishes. The mood is relaxed and the food is satisfying to the soul as well as the palate.

Chef Duke LoCicero hits the high notes of Italy's contributions to the local cuisine at Cafe Giovanni, where he celebrates New World Italian cooking. Adding to the restaurant's emphasis on romance, opera singers perform regularly at the cozy restaurant and bar. He believes in entertaining at all times, with a personality that is larger than his laughter.

Consequently, Chef Duke is a mainstay on radio and television programs.

Chef Duke is a regular fixture on the civic and charitable circuit, offering his many and diverse cooking talents to benefit good causes. The Chef Duke Foundation for Kids, which he created after 2005's Hurricane Katrina, benefits Children's Hospital in New Orleans and other children in difficult medical and financial circumstances.

CAFÉ GIOVANNI
PROSCIUTTO
AND CREOLE CREAM CHEESE PUFFS

Sheets of frozen puff pastry, available in most grocery store freezer departments, are a chef's favorite tool for creating almost any kind of enclosed appetizer. These savory puffs can be created from almost any variety of meats and cheeses with your favorite herbs and seasonings. Let your imagination create your own personal recipe and keep it a secret. Tell no one.

SERVES: 36 small puffs

9 slices	prosciutto	1 package	frozen puff-pastry dough,
2 tablespoons	chopped fresh basil		17.3 ounces, in sheets
4-ounce log	peppered goat cheese		9 inches square
1/4 cup	Creole cream cheese		

*Sour cream, Philadelphia-style cream cheese or other cheese may be substituted.

DIRECTIONS

Preheat the oven to 350°F.

Remove one 9-by-9-inch sheet of pastry dough from the package and defrost it at room temperature. Refreeze the remaining dough for later use.

Divide the pastry sheet into 9 equal squares. Place one piece of prosciutto at the center of each square of dough, folding the prosciutto smoothly to fit within the square.

In a small metal bowl combine the Creole cream cheese and goat cheese and blend well.

Place a heaping tablespoon of the cheese mixture onto each of the 9 pastry squares, on top of the slice of prosciutto. (These 9 pieces will be further divided to yield 36 baked triangular puffs.)

Fold the four corners of the dough inward to form a smaller square, with the sheet's corners meeting at the center. This will cover the filling and create a tidy little package. An alternative method is to place the squares in a greased muffin tin, add the fillings and then fold each corner over the top.

Bake the puffs 15 to 20 minutes until golden brown and remove them from the oven. Then cut each square twice diagonally to create four triangular puffs.

The puffs may be served either warm or at room temperature.

CHEF LEAH CHASE
RED BEAN CANAPÉS

We love our red beans and rice, an old-fashioned Monday wash-day tradition as comforting as Chef Leah Chase's ready smile and embrace. This appetizer takes a novel twist with leftover red beans.

SERVES: 24 canapés

1	loaf of New Orleans-style French bread or a French baguette	1/2 bunch	green onions, whites and green parts, chopped
1	16-ounce can of Blue Runner Creole Cream-style Red Beans*	1 pound	smoked sausage** sour cream for garnish
1 cup	grated cheddar cheese		

*2 cups of cooked red beans, drained and slightly mashed, may be used as a substitute for the canned beans.
** If New Orleans-style smoked sausage is not available, other sausages similar to smoked kielbasa may be used.

DIRECTIONS

Preheat oven to 350°F.

Heat red beans in a small-to-medium size saucepan. Drain any standing liquid and set aside. If using cooked red beans rather than canned ones, mash them slightly so they are creamy but some whole beans can still be seen.

Cook the sausage in a skillet until hot and the skin is beginning to crisp. Cut on a slight diagonal into oblong slices about 1/8 to 1/4-inch thick.

Cut the bread loaf on a slight diagonal into slices 1/2 inch wide and toast them until golden brown.

Spread each toast slice with a layer of red beans about 1/4 to 1/2 inch deep. Add 2 to 3 thin slices of sausage, covering the red beans.

Top with 2 tablespoons of cheese. Return to oven to heat and melt the cheese until bubbling. Remove from oven, add sour cream if desired, garnish with chopped green onion and serve immediately.

Acclaimed restaurateur and chef Leah Chase began her culinary career at the Coffee Pot, an old French Quarter restaurant. It still stands next door to Pat O'Brien's bar on St. Peter Street, and Leah now stands in her own kitchen at Dooky Chase's on Orleans Avenue.

At the Coffee Pot, she was not allowed to cook. "It was before women were welcome in the kitchen," Leah says, "and we were told it was because we couldn't lift a large, full pot, which was beside the point."

When Leah married, she joined her husband at Dooky Chase's restaurant and took command of the kitchen there. She and Dooky expanded the restaurant from a sandwich shop to a New Orleans landmark.

In the interim she has entertained dignitaries from many fields, and from around the world, including more than one president of the United States.

In her mid-80s now, Leah is the acknowledged "Queen of Creole Cuisine" and the city's favorite chef-ambassador, with a smile as generous and as large as her heart.

That's not bad at all for someone who was not allowed to cook in the Coffee Pot's kitchen.

Cochon celebrates the pig in all of its delicious preparations. Opened not long after Hurricane Katrina in 2005, the restaurant quickly captured the affections of fickle New Orleanians. In no time the word spread to visitors, and Cochon rapidly received national attention.

With a wood-burning stove, the co-owners, Chef Stephen Stryjewski and Chef Donald Link, embrace the traditions of Southern cooking, providing hearty, country-style food in casual surroundings. Donald first gained acclaim with his contemporary-New Orleans restaurant, Herbsaint. Stephen graduated from the Culinary Institute of America. Following a tour of restaurants in Europe and California's Napa Valley, he landed in New Orleans.

In 2007 Cochon was nominated for a James Beard Award as one of America's best new restaurants, and Donald received the award as best chef in the country's Southern region. The James Beard Foundation recognizes outstanding achievement in the country's food and wine industry.

COCHON

WATERMELON RIND PICKLES

A southern favorite, these pickles are a cooling accompaniment to any spicy dish or as a nice garnish.

SERVES: One large watermelon makes about a gallon of rind

4 quarts	prepared watermelon rind		1 quart	white vinegar
3 tablespoons	pickling satsuma*		1 quart	water
2 quarts	cold water		1	lemon, thinly sliced
8 cups	sugar			

*Pickling satsuma, which is calcium hydroxide, firms the fruit. It is available at many local markets or online from www.MrsWages.com, an excellent pickling resource. It also can be obtained at pharmacies under the name slaked satsuma or hydrated satsuma.

Make a tied cheesecloth spice bag with the following:

1 tablespoon	whole cloves		1/4 teaspoon	mustard seed
1 tablespoon	whole allspice		3 sticks	cinnamon

DIRECTIONS

A watermelon's green skin never breaks down in pickling, and the pinkish-red flesh becomes mushy and texturally unappealing. So all of the skin and flesh must be removed from the rind.

Dice the rind into 1-inch cubes. Set aside.

Dissolve the pickling satsuma in the 2 quarts of cold water and pour over the rind pieces. If needed, add more water to cover the rind.

Allow the rind to soak 6 hours or overnight.

Pour out and drain the soaking water, then rinse the rind pieces with cold water. Place the rinds in a large, non-reactive pot (made with stainless steel, enamel or glass) and cover with cold water. Cook until tender, about 30 minutes. Drain and set aside.

Combine sugar, vinegar, water and lemon in a large stockpot and bring to a boil over medium- high heat. Add the spice bag and simmer the liquid for 10 minutes.

Add the reserved rind and cook until the rind is transparent, about 2 hours. The rind pieces will go from white to almost glass-like in appearance as they cook. When they become clear, they are done.

To can the pickled rinds, remove the spice bag and pack the rinds and liquid into hot sterilized canning jars, leaving 1/4-inch headspace. Secure the lids and place the jars in boiling water for 10 minutes to create a proper seal.

BARBECUED PORK RIBS

There are several components to this recipe, but the end product is well worth the preparation time to prepare it. It is scaled for four racks of ribs and can easily be adjusted for larger batches with a little more effort. The rib rub can easily be made in larger batches and will hold in an airtight container for a few months.

The barbecue sauce will yield about three cups, more than enough for two or three batches of ribs. The watermelon pickle is also delicious on its own and will last for a year if canned.

Curly's St. Louis-style ribs are used in Cochon's kitchen. They are 2-pound racks trimmed of cartilage and fat. Full racks or baby back ribs will work just fine and are readily available at any supermarket. The ribs are smoked for four hours in a specialized smoker at the restaurant. At home it is easier to cook the ribs in the oven and finish on the grill.

SERVES: 16 as appetizers or 8 as entrées

RIB RUB

This recipe produces a sufficient amount of rub mix to season four racks of ribs. The ingredient measurements are very flexible and can be adjusted to satisfy any taste. The seedless chile-pepper flakes impart more chile flavor and less heat, and the smoked paprika imparts a slight smoky flavor that does not taste artificial.

2 cups	brown sugar	1 teaspoon	ground cayenne
1/4 cup	kosher or sea salt	2 tablespoons	seedless chile-pepper flakes*
2 tablespoons	ground dry mustard	1/2 cup	ground chile powder
1 tablespoon	ground fennel	1 teaspoon	sweet smoked paprika**
3 tablespoons	ground black pepper	1 teaspoon	hot smoked paprika**

*Available at Asian or specialty markets and on the Internet.
**Recommended smoked paprika brand is La Chinata. Regular paprika can be substituted, or the ingredient can be omitted.*

DIRECTIONS

Combine all ingredients and store in an airtight container.

SERVES: 16 as appetizers or 8 as entrées

RIBS

4	racks of pork ribs, about 2 pounds each	1 clove	garlic, chopped
1	batch rib rub	1 tablespoon	honey
1/2 cup	chicken stock	1 recipe	barbecue sauce
			diced watermelon pickles*

See page 78 for watermelon-pickle recipe.

DIRECTIONS

Remove the thin membrane from the bone side of each rack of ribs. This can be done with a dry towel, your fingernails and, most of all, patience. Start in a corner of the rack and scrape the bone with a knife edge until the membrane starts to lift up. Grab the tip of the membrane with a towel and peel it off. The membrane also can be scored by running a knife along the bones. Removing the membrane is worth the extra time. It prevents the ribs from curling up since it never really breaks down in cooking.

Apply the rib rub to the ribs liberally and leave them to marinate in the refrigerator overnight. Preheat the oven to 275°F.

Remove the ribs from the refrigerator and shake off any excess rub and juice that has accumulated. (However, do not rinse the ribs.)

Lay two of the rib racks on a length of aluminum foil long enough for them to be wrapped and sealed. Do not wrap and seal them yet. Repeat with the other two racks. Set aside.

Combine the chicken stock, garlic and honey in a saucepan and bring the liquid to a simmer. When the simmer is reached, pour half of the seasoned stock into each aluminum package and seal it. Cook the packages on a sheet pan in a 275°F oven for 2 to 3 hours or until the meat easily pulls away from the bone. Cool until ready to use or grill immediately.

Grill the ribs until hot over medium-high heat. Apply an even layer of barbecue sauce to the ribs and allow it to caramelize lightly.

Move the ribs to a serving platter and sprinkle a liberal amount of the watermelon pickles over the ribs. Don't skimp on the watermelon pickles; the idea is to offset the spicy barbecue sauce and complement the meaty ribs. You should get some of the sauce and pickle in every bite.

Michael Lauve insists that he is not a cook. However, he is one terrific graphics guy. His fine hand touched every page in New Orleans Classic Appetizers and deftly created a thing of beauty with numerous changes, and tweaking from the other side of the office.

He usually works with a cat asleep on his lap. When he is not at the computer, he is gardening.

New Orleanians are always looking for ways to use Creole tomatoes, past our basic sliced tomato and mayo sandwich, salads, and just plain eaten out of hand warm from the bush or window sill.

Michael grows them in his garden, but those of us without patches of land head to Plaquemines Parish to secure our baskets of Creole beauties from the roadside stands.

MICHAEL LAUVE
CREOLE TOMATO AND ONION TART

.SERVES: 6

TART CRUST

YIELDS: Six 3 1/2 inch pie shells

1 1/2 cups	pastry flour	10 tablespoons	Crisco All-Vegetable Shortening
1 teaspoon	sugar	4 tablespoons	cold whole milk
1/4 teaspoon	kosher or sea salt		

DIRECTIONS

In a mixing bowl, blend together the pastry flour, sugar and salt until well combined. Using a fork or pastry cutter, mix the shortening into the dry ingredients, until the shortening-flour mixture resembles cornmeal. Slowly add the cold milk to the mixture, and mix carefully by hand. Once the dough is formed into a ball, work no longer than 1 minute. Wrap the dough in plastic and refrigerate for an hour before using.

Preheat the oven to 400°F.

Roll the dough out forming a slab 1/4 inch thick. Cut it into six rounds 5 1/2 inches thick and fit them into 3-1/2-inch tart shells that have been well buttered and floured. Line the inside of each tart crust with a piece of aluminum foil and fill with dried beans or rice to weigh down the dough during the cooking process. Place the tart crusts into the preheated oven and bake for 10 to 12 minutes or until the dough is cooked through but not brown. Remove the crusts from the oven. Once they are cool, remove the foil and rice or beans from the crusts and set them aside.

FILLING

3 tablespoons	extra-virgin olive oil	3 medium	vine ripened Creole tomatoes
3 medium	thinly sliced Vidalia or Texas Sweet onions	1 cup	grated Gruyere cheese
1 pinch	sugar		kosher or sea salt to taste
			freshly ground black pepper to taste

DIRECTIONS

Preheat the oven to 400°F.

In a medium-size sauté pan, heat the olive oil or butter over medium heat. Add the onions and the sugar and cover the skillet. Caramelize the onions by allowing them to turn golden, stirring occasionally. This should take about 10 minutes. Remove the onions from the heat and set them aside to cool.

While the onions are cooling, slice the tomatoes to a 1/8-inch thickness. Place the tomato slices on paper towels and sprinkle them lightly with salt to remove excess moisture. Once the onions have cooled slightly, spread them evenly on the bottom of the tart shell. Arrange the tomato slices over the caramelized onions and sprinkle the top with the grated Gruyere cheese.

Place the tarts in the oven, and bake until the cheese is melted and golden, about 25 to 30 minutes. Remove the tarts from the oven and allow them to cool for 3 to 5 minutes before serving.

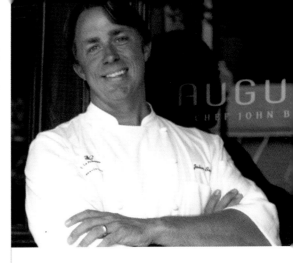

HONEY ISLAND CHANTERELLE TARTS

SERVES: 6 appetizers

TART CRUSTS

YIELD: eight 3-1/2-inch pie shells

1 1/2 cups	pastry flour	10 tablespoons	All-Vegetable Shortening
1 teaspoon	sugar	4 tablespoons	cold whole milk
1/4 teaspoon	salt		

In a mixing bowl, blend together the pastry flour, sugar and salt until well combined. Using a fork or pastry cutter, mix the shortening into the dry ingredients, until the shortening-flour mixture resembles cornmeal. Slowly add the cold milk to the mixture, and mix carefully by hand. Once the dough is formed into a ball, knead no longer than 1 minute. Wrap the dough in plastic and refrigerate for 30 minutes before using. Preheat the oven to 400°F.

Roll the dough out forming a slab 1/4-inch thick. Cut it into 5-1/2-inch rounds and fit them into 3-1/2-inch tart shells that have been well buttered and floured. Line the inside of each tart crust with a piece of aluminum foil and fill the foil with dried beans or rice to weigh down the dough during the cooking process. Place the tart crusts into the preheated oven and bake for 10 to 12 minutes, until the dough is cooked through but not brown. Remove the crusts from the oven. Once they are cool, remove the foil and rice or beans from the crusts and set them aside.

ROYAL FILLING

2	large onions, thinly sliced	9	eggs
2 tablespoons	virgin olive oil	6	tart crusts from previous recipe
1 quart	heavy cream		

Preheat the oven to 350°F. Caramelize the onions in a large skillet over medium heat with the olive oil and a pinch of salt. When the onion slices are golden brown and sweet, remove from them from heat, set them aside and allow to cool.

Heat the cream in a small saucepan. Just before the cream reaches the boiling point, turn off the heat. In a separate, large-size metal bowl beat the eggs until well combined. Slowly add the hot cream while whisking vigorously until it is all combined. Distribute the onions into the tart crusts evenly, and fill with the cream-and-egg mixture. Place the tarts in the preheated oven and bake 15 to 20 minutes, or until the tops of the tarts are golden brown.

LAVENDER-HONEY VINAIGRETTE

1 cup	rice wine vinegar	1	French shallot, minced
4 ounces	lavender honey	1 teaspoon	minced fresh lavender
2 cups	canola oil	3 cups	finely chopped Belgian endive
2 cups	extra-virgin olive oil	2 cups	roughly chopped bacon

Whisk together all of the above ingredients, except the bacon, and season with salt and sugar to taste. Sauté the bacon in a large very hot skillet until browned, then add 1 cup of water. Reduce the mixture until the water evaporates and just the bacon fat remains. Drain and reserve the bacon fat. Set aside, separately, the diced bacon pieces and the bacon fat.

SAUTÉ OF CHANTERELLES

1 tablespoon	bacon fat from previous recipe
1 teaspoon	minced French shallot
1 teaspoon	minced garlic
4 cups	washed fresh Chanterelle mushrooms, or a mixture of seasonal wild mushrooms
1/2 cup	veal demi-glace*

If demi-glace is not available, chicken stock may be substituted, but demi-glace is preferred.

Sauté the mushrooms, with a small amount of the reserved bacon fat and a small pinch of salt, in a large skillet over high heat until golden brown. Add the minced shallot and garlic and sauté for 2 to 3 minutes. Lower the heat to medium. Add the 1/2 cup of demi-glace or chicken stock and simmer for 1 minute. Remove the mushrooms and liquid from heat and set aside.

To serve, first warm the tarts in the oven set at low heat. Then toss the frisée lettuce and the diced bacon with a small amount of honey-lavender vinaigrette. Place the warm tarts on small plates and finish each with a scoop or two of the sautéed mushrooms and a ball of the frisée salad. Top each tart with pieces of the diced bacon.

CHEF TOMMY DiGiovanni
MUSHROOMS VERONIQUE

Mushrooms are another of Mother Nature's little containers. Once the stem is snapped off, the tiny cup begs to be dressed up with almost any savory tidbit, especially crab meat, shrimp, crawfish or oysters. The possibilities are endless, and you're challenged to try almost anything that appeals to your good taste.

The recipe for Mushrooms Veronique is a wonderful combination, and I'd not change a thing if I were to tinker with it. And tinkering is something to do on a lazy afternoon with leftover seafood stuffings and other small amounts of goodies hiding in the refrigerator.

SERVES: 60 bites or 12 appetizers

60	button or small cremini mushrooms, about 1 to 1 1/2 inch in diameter
60	white seedless grapes
15 ounces	(three 5-ounce packages) Boursin Cheese au Poivre at room temperature
1 cup	warm clarified butter
4 cups	grated Parmigiano-Reggiano cheese

DIRECTIONS

Preheat oven to 350°F.

Wipe the mushrooms clean and remove stems.

Before stuffing the mushroom caps, steam them upside down over simmering water for a few minutes, or place in the preheated oven for 5 minutes. Drain. (During steaming the caps, some of their water is released, shrinking them by half and concentrating their flavor.)

Allow the mushrooms to cool, for handling.

Increase the oven temperature to 425°F.

Place one grape in each mushroom cap. Scoop up a bit of Boursin cheese and mound it over the mushroom cap, completely enclosing the grape.

Dip each stuffed mushroom in clarified butter, then dredge in Parmigiano-Reggiano cheese. Shake off excess.

Place the stuffed caps on a sheet pan lined with parchment paper. Bake for 8 to 10 minutes until golden brown.

Arnaud's Executive Chef Tommy DiGiovanni is the champion of this signature dish and we have him to applaud when it is served in the highlights of the sparking beveled glass wall of the main dining room.

CLARIFIED BUTTER

Clarified or drawn butter is simply melted butter with the solids removed. Without these solids, clarified butter withstands high temperatures and maintains the delicate butter flavor.

Over low heat, warm the unsalted butter until it melts. Remove from heat and let stand for a few minutes to allow the milk solids to settle to the bottom.

Pour off the clarified butter into a container. Keep cool.

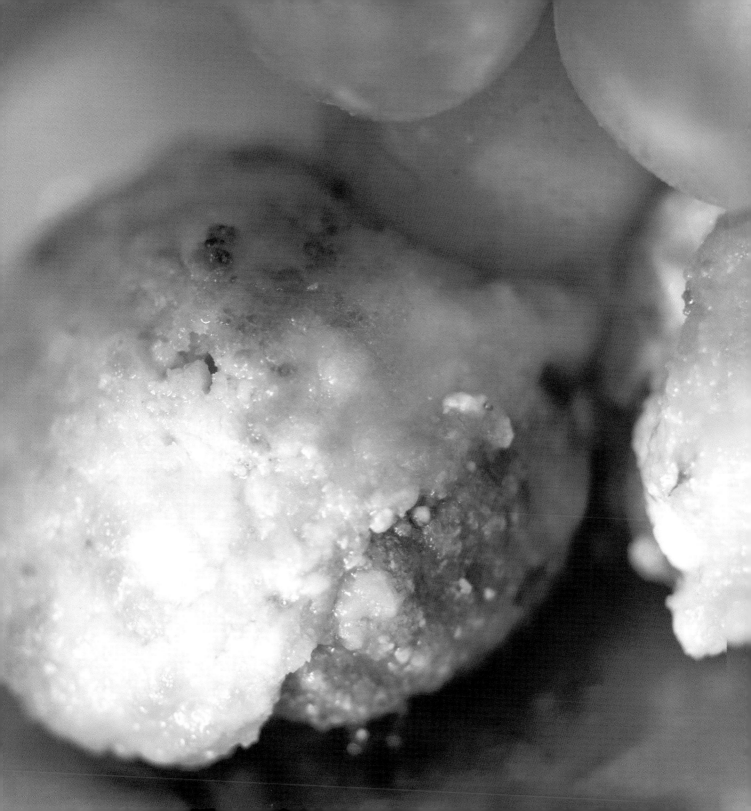

JOEL'S FINE CATERING
Quail Eggs with Caviar

Deviled eggs are one of the best-loved of all egg dishes, but this recipe takes the standard version a step further by using tiny quail eggs nestled in demitasse spoons. The quail eggs taste exactly like hen's eggs, which can be used with this recipe. However, based on the difference in the yolk sizes, hen's eggs would provide for only 6 eggs, or 12 halves. If more are desired, the quantities below can be increased accordingly.

SERVES: 48 BITES

2 dozen	quail eggs	1/4 teaspoon	lemon juice
2 teaspoons	finely diced French shallots		kosher or sea salt, to taste
1/2 teaspoon	Creole mustard		freshly ground black
2 teaspoons	sour cream		pepper, to taste
1 teaspoon	finely chopped chives	3 ounces	choupique caviar*
1 teaspoon	finely chopped chervil, plus chervil sprigs (optional) for garnish		

The choupique is a fish species found in Louisiana's wetlands. If choupique caviar is not available, use other fresh, good-quality caviar or roe. Obviously, caviar atop the stuffed eggs is optional.

DIRECTIONS

In small saucepan place quail eggs in water to cover by 1 inch, and place over medium-high heat. When water starts to steam slowly, stir it until it reaches a boil. Cook eggs for 1 minute. Remove saucepan from heat and place eggs in a colander.

Run cold water over eggs until they are completely cool, about 3 minutes. Gently crack eggs on the side of the pan and remove the shells, taking great care not to damage the whites.

Using a small, sharp knife, cut each egg in half. Remove each yolk with a small spoon and place it in a medium sized bowl. If necessary, use the tip of your knife to collect any yolk that's stuck in the cavity. Set aside the egg-white halves.

In the bowl, mash the yolks with a fork until smooth. Combine the rest of the ingredients and mix thoroughly.

Fill a piping bag or a zipper-lock bag with the egg mixture. (If using a zipper-lock bag, cut a small hole in one corner and use as you would a piping bag). Pipe some of the mixture into each egg-white half until it is just over full.

Before serving, mound the caviar on top the egg and garnish with a sprig of chervil.

Arrange on a serving plate, or place each egg in a demitasse spoon and arrange the spoons in a pinwheel design, in rows or any design that complements the table and service style.

Joel Dondis has created a mini-conglomerate by cooking up creative ideas for Joel's Fine Catering, as well as sophisticated dining at La Petite Grocery restaurant, and decadent pastries and confections at Sucré, a shop in Uptown New Orleans.

A graduate of the Culinary Institute of America in New York, Dondis's European experience complemented his turn at the stoves of Mr. B's Bistro and Emeril's in New Orleans.

Tasteful events for large and small social events keep Joel in the forefront of imaginative catering across the city and around the country with sophistication and elegance, offering a taste of New Orleans with flair and authentic Crescent City flavors.

CHEESE STRAWS

Cheese straws freeze beautifully, stay crisp for a week in a covered container and therefore are usually on hand in a New Orleans kitchen. Hardly any event in this town occurs without cheese straws. They're our answer to quick and easy munchies for both drop-in guests, grand occasions and handy. Certainly other Southern cooks may also claim squatter's rights but we know better and know ours taste better. Fighting words? Probably. Send me your cheese straws (already baked in a covered container) so we can taste them.

SERVES: 4-6 dozen straws, 2 to 2 1/4 inches long

1 cup	grated extra-sharp cheddar cheese
1/2 cup	unsalted butter, room temperature
1 1/2 cups	all-purpose flour
1/2 teaspoon	kosher or sea salt
1/4 teaspoon	cayenne pepper
1/4 cup	Parmigiano-Reggiano paprika to taste
	kosher or sea salt to taste

DIRECTIONS

Preheat oven to 350°F.

In a food processor, pulse cheddar cheese and butter until combined. Add flour, salt, cayenne pepper and Parmigiano-Reggiano cheese and process again until a crumbly dough forms. (The dough should hold together when a handful of it is pressed in your hand.)

Fill either a star-tipped cookie press or pastry bag with the dough and pipe it onto an ungreased, metal cookie sheet in long, parallel strips separated by about 1-1/2 inches. Dark metal cookie sheets tend to allow the cheese straws to brown too quickly.

Cut the long cheese strips into 2 to 2-1/2-inch lengths and separate them slightly with the knife.

Bake for 20 minutes. Do not let the cheese straws brown.

Remove them from the oven and, if desired, sprinkle with salt and paprika while they are warm. Allow the cheese straws to cool on the cookie sheet. Once they are cool, remove them with a spatula.

The cheese straws can be stored for up to one week in an airtight container. They also can be frozen and thawed to room temperature before serving.

Pecan and Blue Cheese Crostini

Crostini is a platform for creativity. Crostini in Italian means, "little toasts." Thinly slicing bread and toasting or grilling so that it becomes crisp makes them ready to be dressed with an assortment of toppings — such as cheeses, tomatoes, olive oil and seasonings. One easy summer treat is crostini rubbed with the cut side of a garlic clove, topped with a tomato slice, drizzled with olive oil and sprinkled with Parmesan-Reggiano cheese, then garnished with fresh basil.

SERVES: 24 pieces

1	baguette of French bread
1/2 pound	blue cheese
6 tablespoons	unsalted butter
6-ounce bag	whole pecans, shelled
2 tablespoons	chopped parsley for garnish

DIRECTIONS

Slice baguette on a bias into 24 equal pieces. Melt 2 tablespoons of the butter in a large skillet over medium heat. Place 12 of the baguette slices face down in the melted butter and toast lightly on one side until golden brown. Remove and set aside. Wipe out the skillet with a paper towel. Add another 2 tablespoons of butter to the skillet and toast the remaining 12 slices. Set aside.

Preheat oven to 300°F

Place pecan halves on a baking sheet and lightly toast them in the oven for 10 minutes or until browned. Remove them from the oven and cool to room temperature.

Using a cheese grater, crumble the blue cheese. Mix well with 2 tablespoons of room temperature butter.

Loosely combine pecans with the blue cheese and butter mixture.

Arrange the 24 toasted baguette slices (or crostini) on a baking sheet. Divide the cheese and pecan mixture equally and mound on top of each crostini.

Place baking sheet in oven to melt the cheese for 5 to 7 minutes, watching carefully until the cheese is softly melted.

Garnish with chopped parsley, if desired, and serve.

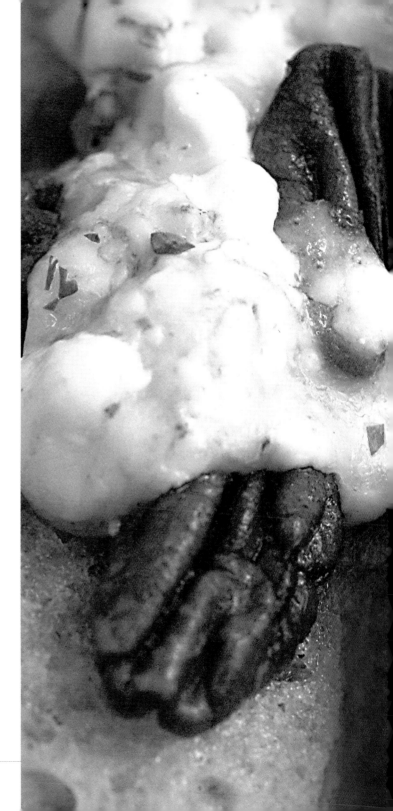

SEASONED FLOUR

YIELD: 2 1/4 cups

2 cups	all-purpose flour
4 tablespoons	paprika
1 tablespoon	kosher or sea salt
1 tablespoon	garlic powder
1/2 tablespoon	freshly ground black pepper
1/2 cup	cayenne pepper

DIRECTIONS

Blend the seasonings with the flour. Store any leftover flour in a covered container.

SEVEN-LAYER DIP

High school or college kids huddled around a TV for a football game could easily tackle this dirt-simple recipe. It requires no stove-top cooking and doesn't make a real mess. If you are from New Orleans, South Louisiana or Texas, this is a familiar-chip-and dip goodie. Your friends will believe you're an incredible cook.

SERVES: 48

1 16-ounce can	refried beans or Louisiana red beans
1 tablespoon	taco seasoning mix
1 cup	shredded cheddar or monterey jack cheese
1 cup	sour cream
1 cup	shredded lettuce
1/2 cup	chopped green onion
2 tablespoons	sliced ripe olives and (to taste) sliced pitted jalepeños, sliced, to taste
1 cup	salsa

DIRECTIONS

In a medium-size bowl, mix refried beans and taco seasoning mix. Using a spatula, spread the bean-and-seasoning mixture on the bottom of a 9-inch pie plate.

Layer remaining ingredients over the bean-and-seasoning mixture, finishing with a layer of salsa.

Cover and refrigerate several hours.

Serve with fresh corn chips.

CREOLE SEASONING

YIELD: 1/2 cup

3 tablespoons	sweet paprika
2 tablespoons	onion powder
2 tablespoons	garlic powder
2 tablespoons	dried oregano leaves
2 tablespoons	dried sweet basil
1 tablespoon	dried thyme leaves
1 tablespoon	freshly ground black pepper
1 tablespoon	freshly ground white pepper
1 tablespoon	cayenne pepper
1 tablespoon	kosher or sea salt
dash	chili powder
dash	cumin powder

In a medium-size mixing bowl, mix dry ingredients together using a fork, or place in jar, cover and shake thoroughly. Store in a tightly sealed container.

For blackened seasoning add an additional tablespoon each of paprika and cayenne pepper.

CREAM CHEESE WITH PICKAPEPPER SAUCE

A friend, a Texan with her boots firmly planted in the kitchen, swears her fellow Texans invented cream cheese with Pickapepper sauce, but we know better. She claims cheese straws, too. Texans are like that. This recipe is no more difficult than opening a block of cream cheese and twisting off a few lids. There is no cooking.

6 ounce package	cream cheese, room temperature
1 bottle	Pickapepper sauce
1 box	crackers of choice
	jellies of choice, optional

DIRECTIONS

Place the block of cream cheese on a serving plate, or whip the cream cheese in a mixer to soften it. Top with a generous amount of Pickapepper Sauce.

For a more colorful version, alternate stripes of brightly colored fruit jellies across the top of the cream-cheese block.

Serve with a basket of crackers.

HOW TO BOIL SHRIMP

2 pounds	medium (21 to 25 to the pound) fresh raw Louisiana shrimp, in shells
1 packet	dry Zatarain's Crab & Shrimp Boil (or 1 tablespoon liquid Zatarain's Crab & Shrimp Boil)
2 quarts	water
2 quarts	ice cubes

Place the dry or liquid seasoning in a large pot of water and bring to a boil. Add shrimp and return to a boil. Set a timer for 2 minutes. When the timer sounds remove the pot from heat.

Add the ice to the pot and stir thoroughly. Let the shrimp stand in the water and seasonings for 1/2 hour. Drain, shell and devein the shrimp. If they are to be served as finger food, leave the shrimp tails on. If serving as an appetizer, remove the tails.

SHRIMP STOCK

| 2 to 3 cups | shrimp shells and heads |
| 3 quarts | water |

Place the shrimp heads and shells in a large pot and cover with the water. Bring to a boil over high heat, then lower the heat and simmer gently until the amount of liquid is reduced to about 2 quarts. Strain through a fine-mesh strainer and freeze in 1-cup increments for later use.

CRAB STOCK

YIELD: 1 quart

2 tablespoons	vegetable oil	1/2 cup	chopped celery
1	small medium onion, chopped	6 cups	water
		5	gumbo crabs*
1/2 cup	chopped leeks, green top part only	1	bay leaf
1 clove	garlic, chopped	1 teaspoon	whole black peppercorns

Gumbo crabs are Louisiana blue crabs that are not large enough for their meat to be harvested. They should be completely cleaned and washed before they are used.

In a 1-gallon stockpot over medium heat, sauté onions, leeks, garlic and celery in the vegetable oil for 3 to 5 minutes. When the onions become transparent, add the water, the gumbo crabs and all other ingredients to the vegetables and simmer for 1 to 1 1/2 hours, occasionally skimming the top to remove impurities throughout the cooking time. Strain the stock to remove any remaining impurities. After allowing the stock to cool, freeze it in 1-cup increments for later use.

CAYENNE BEURRE BLANC

YIELDS: 2 cups

1	large shallot, chopped
1	sprig fresh thyme
1	bay leaf
1 cup	white wine vinegar or champagne vinegar
1/2 cup	white wine
1/2 cup	heavy cream
1/2 pound	butter, unsalted
	salt, to taste
	cayenne pepper, to taste
	paprika, to taste

In a large saucepan over high heat, place the chopped shallot, thyme, bay leaf, vinegar and white wine and bring to a boil.

Reduce the liquid until it reaches a syrup-like consistency. Add the cream and reduce again to 1/3 of the original amount of the syrup-and-cream mixture.

Lower heat to a simmer and slowly whisk in the butter.

Remove from heat and strain through a very fine strainer or a home colander that has been lined with a large paper coffee filter.

To finish, season with salt, cayenne pepper and paprika to taste.

RED REMOULADE SAUCE

YIELDS: 2 cups

1/2 cup	ketchup
1/2 cup	Creole mustard
1 tablespoon	paprika
1 tablespoon	cayenne pepper
1/2 teaspoon	salt
2 tablespoons	fresh lemon juice
1/4 teaspoon	Tabasco
1 cup	olive oil

Combine all ingredients except olive oil in a bowl with a wire whisk. Add the oil a little at a time, whisking until all oil is incorporated. Add a little more mustard or cayenne pepper to taste. Cover and refrigerate.

INDEX

ACKNOWLEDGEMENTS

Of all the people who made this book possible, the chefs and restaurateurs who make New Orleans a great food town are the most important of all.

I'm especially grateful to Chef Robert Barker, our culinary director, who personally checked these recipes and lent a guiding hand throughout the entire book. He taught us quite a bit, above all that chefs don't like to wash dishes. Chef Tommy DiGiovanni also participated in many ways and he will always have my gratitude.

Gene Bourg edited recipes and made them make sense, as an editor should. Christine Mason worked with us for the second time, which we enjoyed. Michael Lauve managed to keep two graphics computers tied up and work with a cat on his lap most of the time. I think Miss Fluffy was attracted by the computer mouse and I know Michael sneaked treats to her.

Dear friends Linda Ellerbee and Rolfe Tessem cheered me onward and offered great support. Bob Rintz, who introduced me to Billy, my husband, was an eager food taster with Anne Benoit adding her opinions.

Jane and Archie Casbarian, Sheila and Steve Bellaire, and Ann and John Casbon did their share of taste-testing and also kept me fed in return.

Once again, the terrific staff at Pelican Publishing went out of their way to make this a smooth and happy project.

Our booksellers are the lifeblood of the business, and enough thanks never seem to go their way. Thank you, thank you.

As this book was completed, my biggest joy arrived in the birth of tiny Sofia Noor Lunat, the first daughter of my niece Michele Barker and her husband Sule Lunat. It was a race between this book and Sofia, altogether a delightful serendipity.

As always, I own any omissions or errors. Please feel free to send any questions or comments to kit@wohlco.com. In return, please don't send any chain e-mails, jokes or solicitations.

Finally, my appreciation and love go to Billy, my husband. Thank you, my prince. You make it possible.